2/24

Heaven's Currency

Dr. Paul Chaloux

Heaven's Currency

A Study of Love

SOPHIA INSTITUTE PRESS
Manchester, New Hampshire

Sophia Institute Press

Box 5284, Manchester, NH 03108

1-800-888-9344

www.SophiaInstitute.com

Sophia Institute Press is a registered trademark of Sophia Institute.

paperback ISBN 979-8-88911-160-3

ebook ISBN 979-8-88911-161-0

Library of Congress Control Number: 2023949259

First printing

To my family,

who have taught me the meaning of love,

and all who have helped me on my journey.

CONTENTS

ACKNOWLEDGMENTS

I WANT TO ACKNOWLEDGE that Sue Chaloux, Jim Ball, Sr. Mary Catherine Blanding, Allison Brown, John Halligan, Garrett Johnson, and Colleen Lang critiqued and contributed insight to the original draft of this book. Thank you for your aid in making this the best it could be.

Heaven's Currency

INTRODUCTION

HEAVEN'S CURRENCY: A STUDY OF LOVE is the third book in a series that I never expected to write. My journey began as an engineer in upstate New York, developing processes to manufacture computer chips for IBM. I was also a longtime catechist at my local parish church when I encountered an improbable series of events that culminated in a very vivid dream that motivated me to quit my lucrative job and pursue a doctorate in catechetics to "teach the teachers."

Following these unlikely events, I was diagnosed with Parkinson's disease after quitting my job, selling my house, buying a new house in Arlington, Virginia, with my brother, taking on care responsibility for my mother, and accepting a position as a doctoral student at the Catholic University of America. My new neurologist suggested (almost insisted) that I change my course of study to why people suffer. I was shocked that a medical doctor would ask me to change my field of study, but it did intrigue me enough to investigate it in my doctoral studies. Five years later, I successfully defended my dissertation: "The Grace Concealed in Suffering: Developing Virtue and Beatitude."

Over the next year, I rewrote this work three times before it was published by Sophia Institute Press as *Why All People Suffer: How a Loving God Uses Suffering to Perfect Us*. The book was well received, prompting a follow-up, *Dying without Fear*, which reflected a new phase in my life, when the effects of Parkinson's disease were becoming more pronounced and my mother died after a long battle with dementia. This gave me the impetus and the experience to expand on the theology of suffering I developed to focus on death, which is what gives suffering meaning. I found the research, prayer, and contemplation were cathartic for me as I progressed from suffering to dying, and I felt others could benefit from these insights as well.

Dying without Fear also serves another purpose. I have been interested in my family tree for years. I used the true stories of my family to demonstrate that, even with some very hard lives and deaths, you can see in retrospect how God brought about good. These experiences, described in a very vivid narrative, are meant to resonate with readers who have suffered the loss of a loved one, or even those who are dying themselves. As an ethicist, I also gave advice on how to navigate the many moral dilemmas facing the terminally ill. Furthermore, I offered practical counsel on maximizing one's last days and the dying process in general.

This book, *Heaven's Currency*, is a direct outgrowth of the first two books and particularly the latter. When I first penned the line "Love is eternal currency that cannot be lost or stolen, and it is the only thing you can take with you when you die," I knew immediately that it was a compelling thought. Taken superficially, it is easy to understand that we do not cease to love people who have died, and according to the creedal principle of communion of the saints, the souls in Heaven and Purgatory continue to love and pray for us, as noted in the *Catechism of the Catholic Church* (CCC 955).

A study of love and its role in God's plan, however, involves much more than unending love. In many ways love is linked to suffering and death, and so it is a natural extension from my previous two studies. After all, love is as mysterious as suffering and death, though love is the only one of the three states that anyone wants to experience. As I delved into the mystery of love with more rigor, it became clear that to learn about love is to learn to live as God intended, which begins with Him. To search for love is to search for God.

As with my previous two books, *Heaven's Currency* is based heavily on the *Catechism of the Catholic Church* and Sacred Scripture, as well as the great works of the Catholic tradition, particularly Pope Benedict XVI's encyclical *Deus Caritas Est*, St. Thomas Aquinas's *Summa Theologica*, and Pope St. John Paul II's *Salvifici Doloris*.

The book begins with this introduction because I believe the reader deserves to know where the author is coming from. It moves on to the theology of truth, which is included to demonstrate that what is written is credible. From there, I discuss what we know about the four last things (death, judgment, Heaven, and Hell) and the Last Day and how these teachings make God's intentions and plan clearer and easier to follow. The teachings on the Last Day and the last four things also give us hope and the perspective that God has our best interests at heart and will extend His love and mercy to all who seek to follow Him in good faith. This is the key insight that drove all three books.

The rest of the book builds on this base, explaining what the Church has taught about the nature of love and how it fits in God's plan. Learning how to love is a search for human perfection, to become like God so we can live with Him in eternal joy and fulfillment. I explain that we can learn to love in a number of ways, part of God's plan to make it accessible to all. For instance, we can learn from the loving relationships that have existed from the earliest days, including spousal love, parental love, and brotherly love. We can learn to love as Jesus did by following the Beatitudes. We can follow the Ten Commandments, as Jesus advised the rich young man (Matt. 19:17), and we can carry out the works of mercy, which Jesus told us were necessary for entering Heaven (Matt. 25:31–46). Unsurprisingly, the topic of love has been written about extensively by such Church luminaries as St. Paul, St. Thomas Aquinas, St. Thérèse of Lisieux, and most recently, Pope Benedict XVI, and their views have been included as well.

My goal in writing this book was to synergize all these various inputs, giving the reader a clearer understanding of how we must share in the divine nature, learning to love with sufficient intensity to gain entrance into God's Kingdom. There are some "hard cases" explicitly explored with these principles to demonstrate how they are used and to give people hope that God is actively pursuing the salvation of every person. It is not my intention to judge anyone. I merely intend to present the facts as I have come to know them and let people judge for themselves whether the facts are worthy of belief and whether they need or want to take any specific actions in their lives based on what is presented.

One final thought before we take up the subject in earnest. Catholic teaching is clear that no one can get to Heaven on their own and that no one is guaranteed to enter Heaven. However, this is not a reason for despair. Jesus told us that God wants nothing more than to unite with us in Heaven and that He is merciful, forgiving the prodigal son that wasted half his property on a life of dissolution. But God has perfectly balanced judgment and mercy, to help us to grow in love and holiness. He will forgive any sins that we confess with a contrite heart. This mercy allows us to get to Heaven. However, we will be held accountable for any sins that we are not sorry for or have not confessed, and God will certainly not condone mortal sins, which are grave offenses against Him. This is justice and provides the motivation for spiritual growth.

It is, in the end, a matter of attitude. If we love God and trust that everything He does is for our salvation, we will follow His direction as best we are able. When we fall out of grace, we will use the sacrament of Reconciliation to express our sorrow and regain God's graces. This is not too much to ask for eternal joy. In fact, considering that we owe everything to God, including our skills, interests, resources, and very existence, and that He is the source of everything good, true, and beautiful in the world, why wouldn't we love Him? This book will help you understand charity (love of God) and how to increase its intensity by following His direction. It will also be an eye-opener for many people, who will be shocked to understand what self-giving love really means and what it requires them to do. I confess to being one of those people. Nevertheless, put your trust in God and make your best effort, knowing that He loves you and that He does nothing without our salvation in mind.

This book is very much the culmination of the trilogy of God's mysteries. God's plan has become clearer to me through this three-year course of study and with the increasing focus of each stage of my journey, which is documented in these three books. God's plan is magnificent, with all the pieces fitting together and leading to salvation. Suffering and death lead us to love, and the search for love is a search for God. God's love for man is seen throughout and also in every life, if you know what to look for. I understood this better and better throughout this journey, and if you have been taking this journey with me, I hope you have come to the same conclusion. I have written *Why All People Suffer*, *Dying without Fear*, and *Heaven's Currency* to be stand-alone books, but I think the reader will benefit from reading the trilogy in the order it was written to experience the growth in revelation as I experienced it. Indeed, after I learned the meaning of suffering and death in God's plan, I was ready to see them as manifestations of God's deep love for mankind and to recognize that it is by our acceptance and sharing of this love that we build up Heaven's currency within us.

CHAPTER I

UNDERSTANDING TRUTH

Most adult Americans have pondered the big existential questions concerning evil, suffering, and death.[1] These questions have all been definitively answered and are part of the Deposit of Faith (the body of revealed truth in Sacred Scripture and Sacred Tradition) held by the Magisterium of the Church (the Pope and his fellow bishops). Sadly, many in our secular society, including some Catholics, seem oblivious to the truth, as evidenced by a somewhat recent Pew Research Center poll.[2] Perhaps there exists a reluctance or even resistance to understanding the difference between truth and opinion that is driving this. In any case, I will be showing that the *Catechism of the Catholic Church* and the official Church documents are trustworthy, thus clarifying that what has been revealed to the Church can be passed on to the world with confidence.

The truth is not developed by men; rather, it is the outcome of God's plan to be discovered by men for their use. Truth is what is real and is a solid foundation to build upon. The truth is unchangeable

---

[1] Pew Research Center, "Few Americans Blame God or Say Faith Has Been Shaken amid Pandemic, Other Tragedies," November 23, 2021, https://www.pewresearch.org/religion/2021/11/23/few-americans-blame-god-or-say-faith-has-been-shaken-amid-pandemic-other-tragedies/.

[2] Ibid. The Pew Research Center poll also reveals the great misunderstanding of basic Church teaching by some Catholics on questions such as "Is there a Heaven?"

and consistent everywhere. Found through reason and logic, the truth is best understood in light of Jesus Christ and His Church.

Opinion is developed by men who either do not know the truth or oppose it. They seek to act on their opinion instead of the truth. Eventually, these individuals will find that opinion contradicts what is real. The length of time before an opinion conflicts with the truth, or the extent of the confliction, depends on many variables, the most important being how far the opinion strays from the truth. This is why, when the truth is not known, people often seek out expert testimony, in the hopes that an authority can at least come close to the truth and his opinion can be acted on without wide variations in the real world.

Opinions, regardless of the expertise of the authority behind them, cannot replace the truth. Truth is always unchanging and accurate. Science is one methodology for discovering what is true. It is a technique for separating the impacts of variables from each other to isolate the contributions of one particular source. Used correctly, the scientific method can determine what something is made of, what its capabilities are, and how it reacts with other things. Science is useless, however, in discovering God's intentions, which drive every existential question. These must be revealed by God.

To help God's children know the truth, Christ founded His Church and commissioned her to teach all the nations what He has taught them (Matt. 28:18–20). One of the Magisterium's roles is to collect what has been revealed and to transmit it to all generations. Neither the Church nor anyone else can change what is true because the truth is eternal and unchangeable, and Christ is "the way and the truth and the life" (John 14:6). The Church teaches that all public revelation by God ceased at the death of the last apostle (St. John) around the year 100 (CCC 66). The Magisterium can expand the world's understanding of God's designs by testing new insights against known truths. This process, in addition to science and divine revelation, uses reason and logic. If a new insight, from whatever source, is found consistent with all other known truths, it is reliably true. The Magisterium, the teaching arm of the Catholic Church, has recognized thousands of known truths through this process, all of which are shown to align with the Deposit of Faith, making it infinitely believable because of the number and breadth of synergistic truths.

This process has been used for centuries and can reliably be used to evaluate scientific assumptions or even proposed cases of revelation. What is thought to be true will be proven true if it is consistent with all truths. At the same time, false ideas, even highly popular ones, are readily debunked by this process.

Take for example Rabbi Harold Kushner's theology in his popular book *When Bad Things Happen to Good People*. Kushner was writing in the aftermath of his fourteen-year-old son Aaron's death from a genetic abnormality that made him age prematurely. The aggrieved rabbi found himself questioning what he had always held as true. This included three statements that he adapted from the book of Job:

1. God is all-powerful.

2. God is righteous, giving people what they deserve.

3. Rabbi Kushner and his son were good people, not deserving of such harsh treatment.[3]

Since these three beliefs could not be held true simultaneously, Kushner had a logic problem: one or more of his statements were false. Being sure of his and his son's basic goodness and the righteousness of God, Kushner chose to discard the truth that God had enough power to cure his son. Instead, he opined that God does not have the power to change a person's fate. Even though the statement rejecting God's power has enjoyed ongoing popularity for more than forty years, logic

---

[3]   Harold S. Kushner, *When Bad Things Happen to Good People* (New York: Avon Press, 1981), 37.

reveals it to be inconsistent with the truth. First, saying that God, the Creator of all things, is not powerful enough to heal Kushner's son is inconsistent with known truth, especially considering Jesus Christ's healing ministry.[4] Second, the concept of God being beholden to fate clashes with His role as Creator of the universe.

This is not to suggest that Rabbi Kushner and his disciples were wrong about everything or that his work was without value. In fact, his writings have maintained the belief in a just God at a time when many doubted the existence of God. Still, Rabbi Kushner's logic failed because he did not believe in an afterlife, which thus prevented him from seeing his son's illness as having a higher meaning than his earthly suffering would indicate.

Ironically, the truth that Kushner denied, God being all-powerful, is the only statement in Kushner's triad that was true as written. Kushner's belief that God is righteous, giving people what they deserve, erroneously ignores God's mercy. The better statement is that God is love, giving people what is best for them, often more than they deserve but also not what they expect. Kushner's third statement declared that he and his son were good people, undeserving of such harsh treatment. The good rabbi, who obviously studied the book of Job, failed to realize that suffering is not necessarily a punishment for evil — and therefore is not a judgment on whether the sufferer is a good person. Indeed, Job suffered *because* he was righteous and has served God by being as example for others of redemptive suffering (Job 1:8).

Our understanding of the answers to the existential questions (those covering suffering, evil, and death) has an undeniable effect on how we know ourselves and conduct our lives. Understanding these

---

[4]   Christians recognize that God the Son healed people at least sixteen times in the Gospel of Matthew, so to suggest that God, the Creator of the universe, could not heal Kushner's son is inconsistent with Scripture.

deep questions correctly begins with the correct knowledge of God and His relationship with us. This understanding then extends to our view of suffering and justice, the afterlife, and our pursuit of holiness. If we do not understand God's plans properly, then we can easily be misled. Instead of experiencing joy and happiness, we now plunge into confusion, frustration, depression, and despair (CCC 1501–1502).

Getting to Heaven is a unique journey for every soul because we are all unique individuals made specifically by God with the skills and resources necessary to succeed in the roles God has planned for us. As described in the parable of the Prodigal Son (Luke 15:11–32), part of this plan involves returning to the Father's house in Heaven. However, this is not preordained. God respects our autonomy and gives us the opportunity to choose to act in a way that will lead us to spend eternity with Him or without Him. God has perfect foresight and knows which path we will choose. But the choice remains ours to make. No one is predestined to Hell, because that would oppose God's love and His word. St. Paul reminds St. Timothy that God "wills everyone to be saved and to come to the knowledge of the truth" (1 Tim. 2:4).

The journey to Heaven begins with a search for the truth. The Church recognizes that man, while being fully capable of knowing God and His plan from the created world by the natural light of human reason, faces many difficulties in doing so without God revealing Himself. Therefore, man must humbly surrender to God, especially since his senses, imagination, and disordered appetites, the consequences of Original Sin, have impaired his grasp of the truth (CCC 36–37).

The Church further declares that "men in such matters easily persuade themselves that what they would not like to be true is false or at least doubtful" (CCC 37). This is why man stands in need of being enlightened by God's revelation (CCC 38). It is important that men remain open to the teachings of the Catholic Church, the oldest and largest organization on earth and the Church founded by Christ.

The Catholic Church received the charter by the risen Christ to make disciples of all nations, baptizing them in the name of the Father and of the Son and of the Holy Spirit, teaching them to observe all He has commanded His apostles (Matt. 28:19–20).

Our understanding of the key existential questions begins with the truths we are exposed to, because those truths must be consistent with the new truths we surmise. Had Rabbi Kushner recognized that God is a loving God, who uses suffering to lead people to Him rather than to punish them (and that He is all-powerful), then Kushner would have come to a very different revelation concerning his son's illness. He might have seen that his son's death could have led to the salvation of others, and his book would have had a different message and a different conclusion. As it is, Kushner misunderstood his opinion for the truth, which left him with a diminished view of God and no plausible reason his son had to suffer so severely. He was content that his solution meant that neither he nor God was to blame, and this view was popular enough to sell four million books. Yet it failed the ultimate test of any credible theological system: Can it answer all questions consistently and simultaneously? When we find the truth, it will be aligned with all other truths and will apply in this world and the next, allowing us to understand how to live effectively in each.

Because God is the Creator of the universe, we could try to surmise the truth from our experience of His creation through logic and reason. But we could easily be misled by our own expectations and false truths. For instance, Epicurus, the ancient Greek philosopher, was a hedonist, believing that man's greatest goods are comfort and pleasure. He believed that a good and all-powerful God would destroy evil and suffering because they disrupted the goods he most esteemed. Since suffering continues, Epicurus assumed there could be no God.[5]

---

[5] David Konstan, "Epicurus," *The Stanford Encyclopedia of Philosophy*, Summer 2018 edition, ed. Edward N. Zalta, https://plato.stanford.edu/

Epicurus did not witness Jesus Christ rise from the dead as Christians did, so he did not believe in an afterlife. Without the truth of an afterlife, he did not understand that there were greater goods than could be experienced on earth or that God could have more elevated goals than human comfort. In short, he didn't account for the spiritual life. The idea that suffering and death could be used for the benefit of mankind was unfathomable to Epicurus and millions of others before and after him. As we saw earlier, this was also the case for Rabbi Kushner. The Christian answers to these existential questions lead to a loving, all-powerful Creator of the universe, who created man in His own image to share in His life (CCC 306–307).

God has slowly revealed His plan to His people — first through His works and then by sending His Son to testify on His behalf (CCC 65). Without the testimony of Christ and His Church, we could never fully understand God's plan or live in a way that results in our salvation, which is to share in God's life forever. He explicitly taught us to love as He did, which results in joy, and He explained it in several different ways to appeal to all.

Indeed, the Church teaches that God became man for four reasons:

1. By His Passion and Cross, Jesus reconciled us with the Father, paying the debt for all the sins of humanity (CCC 457). This opened Heaven for humanity.

2. Jesus also came to demonstrate the Father's love for mankind, willingly sacrificing Himself for our good (CCC 458). This demonstrated redemptive suffering.

3. He came to be our model of holiness, teaching us how to partake of the divine nature, loving as God loves (CCC 459). This resulted in the Beatitudes.

archives/sum2018/entries/epicurus/.

4. The only-begotten Son of God took flesh to make us partakers of the divine nature (2 Pet. 1:4) As St. Irenaeus memorably describes it, "God became man so that we might become God" (CCC 460). In other words, we could aspire to divinity.

Jesus explains God's vision for humanity in the parable of the Prodigal Son (Luke 15:11–32). This parable begins with a son asking his father for his inheritance immediately rather than receiving it after his father's death. Nevertheless, the father grants his son's wish. The son collects his property and moves to a foreign land, where he wastes his money on a life of dissipation. Finding himself hungry and destitute, he hires himself out to a local pig herder. He learns quickly that he cannot support himself. His hunger intensifying, he comes to the realization that at his father's house everyone is provided for. He resolves to return home, but recognizing that his father might disown him for squandering his inheritance, he develops a plan to humble himself, renouncing his sonship and asking to be treated as a servant.

The son returns home and is surprised to find his father waiting by the side of the road. As soon as he sees his son, the father runs to him and, overjoyed, embraces him. The shocked son launches into his prepared speech, but the father cuts him off, ordering his servants to dress his son in the finest robe and to set up a huge celebration because "this son of mine was dead, and has come to life again; he was lost, and has been found" (Luke 15:24).

Even for someone without scriptural training, this parable is not hard to interpret. God is the father and we, collectively, are the prodigal son. We are lost as a species because Adam, the first man, turned away from God to pursue his own interests (Gen. 3). What is more, it is suffering — from hunger, in this case — that causes the son's return to his father's house.

Like the father in the parable, God loves us and wants nothing more than for us to return home to Him. His love for us never diminishes, regardless of our sinfulness. His love is unconditional and unwavering. What matters to Him is that we repent of our sins and freely choose to live with Him. Like the wise father in the parable, God is willing to let us learn for ourselves the benefits of His way of life versus the alternatives, and like in the parable, it will be our suffering that will tell us which of the alternatives is best, sending us home to God.

Forgiveness without repentance is worthless because it changes nothing and allows error to propagate. In the same way, if our sins were held against us, even after we repented, the motivation to repent would be less effective. Thus, understanding the balance between God's justice and mercy is critical to our spiritual growth. Through His mercy, God meets each man "where he is" and directs him through His laws to live according to His will. Through suffering, God makes His laws fully apparent even to people who do not have access to written versions of the law. When they rebel against the good He has planned for them, or do not use it properly, they will encounter suffering. In fact, suffering is consistent in its application and is a good arbiter of God's will. As discussed in *Why All People Suffer*,[6] there are four tasks of suffering leading us from sin to salvation: (1) to teach proper self-love by creating feedback loops to motivate us to trade vice for virtue, (2) to reorient the soul to God, (3) to unleash our love of neighbor, and (4) to redeem the sufferer who is willing to suffer for the good of another. In this way, God uses suffering to intensify our ability to love and to bring us to eternal life.

SHARING THE DIVINE NATURE

God made man in His image so that man could eventually become like Him and share in His life of eternal joy (*CCC* 457). He established

---

[6] Paul Chaloux, *Why All People Suffer: How a Loving God Uses Suffering to Perfect Us* (Manchester, NH: Sophia Institute Press, 2021), 21–62.

the entire universe for man's benefit, giving us the power to share in the carrying out of His plan (*CCC* 299, 306). God entrusted us with the responsibility of "'subduing' the earth and having dominion over it" (*CCC* 307) while experiencing both good and evil so we can fairly discern if we want to lead the Christian life forever in His Kingdom or would rather choose to do things our way, permanently separated from God. Once we realize that this is what is happening, we will understand that God loves us, and that suffering is not a curse but a compass to help us find our way back to Him (*CCC* 307).

As discussed above, God's balance of love and mercy are critical for the motivation of growth and spiritual evolution in man. These are manifested in the four last things (death, judgment, Heaven, and Hell), which shows the wisdom of God's plan.

CHAPTER 2

THE FOUR LAST THINGS

Providence, God's plan for man's salvation, depends on the four last things (death, judgment, Heaven, and Hell). They call all people to conversion, providing meaning and purpose to our lives (*CCC* 1041). If there was not life after death with an external, authoritative judgment with real consequences, then life would be devoid of meaning. There is a discrete order to the four last things that provides this meaning.

Death

Death is the necessary first step in the four last things, the ending of life on earth. Death is the only one of the four last things that the living have direct access to, and therefore, its existence and inevitability are well documented. However, the existence of death does not mean that everyone accepts its inevitability or that God is the Lord of life. For instance, Sir Francis Bacon, an early proponent of the scientific method, prosed as its goal the preservation of life.[7] This set up a parallel track where people turned to medicine for relief rather than to the promises of Christ when they face death. Virtually everyone, me included, seeks out a cure when they are ill, but there comes a time when it becomes clear that there is not a proven medical answer to the problem. Despite the fabulous improvements in treatment technology, everyone still dies.

---

[7]   Allen Verhey, *The Christian Art of Dying: Learning from Jesus* (Grand Rapids, MI: Eerdmans, 2011), 28–29.

There are both philosophical and theological reasons for death. The universal design depends on death. A finite universe such as ours depends on death to supply resources for new life and even new growth of existing life. Without death, nothing would stop the population from exploding and all available resources from being consumed. This would create a paradox, since everyone has to eat to live and, without death, eventually food would run out, causing death. Without death, there would be no gateway to judgment or to Heaven and Hell, which motivates us to treat others with justice and love.

It is hard to think of a world without death, but it seems certain that it would be less enjoyable than the present earth and far short of the promises of Heaven. In fact, without death, it is easy to envision many different forms of dystopias, with less love, more crowds, and a greater stratification of society and widespread terror, as the powerful would accumulate the remaining resources; over time, there would be boredom as well, as those in power ran out of things to interest them. Man would create his own Hell on earth, where he would live without God and all the benefits of divine law and order.

In today's secular society, the theological aspects of death are rarely, if ever, discussed. Although most people die in hospitals, the emphasis is clearly on finding a medical cure rather than preparing the dying for death. Yet, as death approaches, people naturally become concerned with the particulars of their own death — when it will come, how it will feel, and what will happen after it.

From an individual's standpoint, the timing of our deaths is managed by God's plan and likely involves several factors. One is our readiness to enter Heaven. The book of Wisdom states that some people die young after pleasing the Lord, thus sparing them from future temptation (Wisd. 4:7–11). In the same way, it makes sense that a loving God may extend some people's lives until they find Him.

Our interaction with others may also play a role in the timing of our deaths. There may be situations where our death is impactful for

His plan. Some people die memorable deaths that save souls, others die atrocious deaths that serve as a warning for those around them. Either way, death has a unique role in divine providence. For example, children with fatal disabilities live short lives because their mission in life is to teach their parents to love unconditionally, and after they have completed their mission, they are called home by God, ending their suffering.

Some seek to control God or simply distrust His benevolence by taking their own lives, but this is regrettable because the act of suicide, when committed willingly and with full knowledge, separates us permanently from God (*CCC* 2280–2283). On the other hand, some people go to extraordinary lengths to stay alive, such as freezing their bodies in hopes of future technology reviving them. Technology will never save them; only Jesus can save them and only if they are willing to follow Him. Indeed, God remains the Lord of life for all generations (*CCC* 2280).

If we trust in Christ and His Church, our mindset ought to be much different than those of individuals who do not know God. While others will lament their degradation and dependency, we can see these breakdowns in our bodies as signs of this world's limitations and God's promise of eternal life. We will be motivated to seek out the higher things, rather than wasting our time, energy, and resources on attaining material goods that will vanish with the existing world order on the Last Day (if they even last that long) (*CCC* 1024).

We know that love is the eternal currency that cannot be lost or stolen, and it is the only thing you can take with you when you die. That gives us solace, ensuring us of the continued love from those we leave behind and the ones who died before us. But the greatest source of solace is seeing God face-to-face, which provides everything a human could desire (*CCC* 2548). The hope of the Beatific Vision and the love of God are the reasons we do not fear death. Without faith, hope, and charity, the theological virtues, fear abounds, as the best that exists without God is the unspeakable boredom of eternal nothingness.

JUDGMENT

The Church is clear about what happens after death. "Death puts an end to human life as the time open to either accepting or rejecting the divine grace manifested in Christ" (CCC 1021–1022). At the moment of death, each person will receive his or her particular judgment and, as a consequence, either eternal reward or eternal condemnation. Judgment provides the motivation for righteous living, the treatment of others with love and respect.

Judgment requires death to precede it — otherwise the judgment will be incomplete. Judgment works best in the presence of two distinct choices: in this case, Heaven or Hell. God's presence or absence is the key difference between the choices. There can be no middle ground.

In the end, it is our choice whether we reach Heaven or Hell, whether we accept God's gracious invitation to eternal happiness or spurn Him through mortal sin. As seen in the parable of the Prodigal Son, God awaits our return with open arms. You may ask why anyone would choose Hell, or even why a good God would allow such a place to exist. But God loves and respects us enough to let us freely choose Him or reject Him. He gives us a lifetime to make this decision. God also allows evil and suffering to expose us to life without Him to help us to choose.

Many of us choose sin over God's love, resulting in more suffering. Every time we pursue material wealth over eternal wealth, we are choosing a lesser good over a greater one (the definition of sin).[8] Every time we refuse to serve our neighbor, causing him to suffer instead of alleviating his suffering, we imitate Satan. If we have the

---

[8] *Summa Theologica* (*ST*) I-II, q. 75, art. 1.

mentality that there are no consequences for our actions, then we are tacitly choosing Hell over Heaven. People who end up in Hell are both foolish, in thinking that they deserve what is not rightfully theirs, and arrogant, in thinking they can control like-minded neighbors. The greatest punishment in Hell is being deprived forever of God's presence and protection (*CCC* 1035). The second great punishment is spending eternity with people and demons who will torment you rather than love you.

When I started this book, I thought everyone would be motivated by the promise of Heaven, given that everyone there practices self-giving love. This was doubly true when people consider the horrors of Hell, where everyone looks out only for themselves and cares nothing for their neighbors' well-being. I have come to understand, however, that self-centered people are not frightened by the horrors of Hell. At the same time, most selfish people do not find the promises of Heaven appealing, since God demands self-denial as a prerequisite.

In the parable of the Prodigal Son, many focus on Jesus' portrayal of God as the merciful and loving father. But the character of the prodigal son, who represents us in the parable, is also worth exploring. We are shown that the son rebels against the father and his way of life, demands his future share of the inheritance before he has rights to it, and then departs with it to a distant land, without so much as a thought for his father until he loses everything and is reduced to suffering from starvation. Even then, his only thought is to be comfortable. He does not seem to care to be reunited with his father, and he clearly does not recognize the kindness and love his father showed him. In fact, he is prepared to renounce his sonship and be treated as a servant, and he is surprised by his father's loving actions.

It seems that the only reason the son wanted to go home was his previous experience in his father's home and the promise of something better than he was experiencing. Clearly, the prodigal son did not appreciate his father's intense love for him, nor did he reciprocate that love. The relationship meant much more to the father than to the son. We cannot help but see the self-centeredness of the son and think that the father deserved a lot more love and gratitude, given how much he loved his son and how much he sacrificed for him. The son never bothered to know his father, so he did not come home to be with his father. The son came home to escape his suffering.

We also face a similar situation in regard to Heaven. Do we want to go to Heaven because it is a better place, a world without suffering, or do we want to be with our heavenly Father? For those who do not truly know or love God, the answer is obvious: they want to go to Heaven because they heard it's better than earth. But for those prodigal sons and daughters who resent God's rules and authority, Heaven does not appeal to them. They fail to see that God's love, manifested by His guidance and rules, makes Heaven what it is.

Indeed, order brings joy and happiness to Heaven. What they crave, unfettered personal freedom, only leads to a world of exploitation and anarchy, ruled by those who wield the most power. In contrast, God's will, which recognizes the common good, results in true freedom for all.

Traffic laws provide a simple analogy concerning the importance of order. If everyone drove at their desired speed in the direction of their choice, then many accidents would occur, resulting in great delays. It is by restricting the flow of traffic to one side of the road at a safe speed, and in a given order through intersections, that all drivers have the chance to excel and get to where they are intending to go. Order creates protection and efficiency.

It is not a coincidence that sin is defined as a disordered choice, the choosing of a lesser good over a greater good. Such a choice defies justice and common sense. It can be caused by erroneous judgment, no judgment at all, or even malice (deliberately trying to be disruptive to gain a competitive advantage). Whatever the reason, disorder is opposed to the common good and to God's will.

Heaven and Hell are an integral part of the American psyche. In recent polling, the vast majority (82 percent) of Americans, regardless of professed faith, expressed belief in an afterlife, with virtually all of them believing in Heaven (more than 90 percent) and most believing in both Heaven and Hell (more than 75 percent).[9] But almost 40 percent of those who believe in Heaven failed to mention that Heaven entailed meeting God. Like the prodigal son in the parable, they seem more concerned with eliminating their suffering than being with a loving God. It is God's rules and mercy that eliminate needs and, with that, suffering, because without God, all that remains is need and suffering, the very conditions of Hell. Many fail to enter God's Kingdom because they have sought the creation of God, not the Creator. Only God Himself can bring true happiness through His love and His designs.

Sadly, 25 percent of American adults do not believe in Hell. Their disbelief will not keep them from Hell, and likely will increase their chances of spending eternity there since they will lack some of the motivation to pursue the faith and love required to avoid Hell in favor of at least making it into Purgatory, and the promise of Heaven.

THE LAST DAY

The Church teaches that the universe will end on the final day of history. On that day, Jesus will come in His glory to judge the living and the dead (CCC 1038). The resurrected dead (the just and the unjust)

---

[9] Pew Research Center, "Views on the Afterlife," November 23, 2021, https:// www.pewresearch.org/religion/2021/11/23/views-on-the-afterlife/
    Note 74 percent of Americans believe in Heaven, 61 percent believe in both Heaven and Hell. A total of 82 percent believe in an afterlife, so more than 90 percent of those that believe in an afterlife believe in Heaven and 75 percent believe in both Heaven and Hell.

will gather before Christ, along with the living, on the Last Day. Jesus will separate them one from another as a shepherd separates the sheep from the goats (Matt. 25:31–46). In the presence of Christ, the truth of each person's relationship to God will be laid bare, with the consequences of the person's actions or inactions shown to them (CCC 1039). Based on this, the unjust will be sent away to eternal punishment and the righteous to eternal life (CCC 1038).

"At the end of time, the Kingdom of God will come in its fullness. After the universal judgment, the righteous will reign forever with Christ, glorified in body and soul." At this time, the universe will be renewed, along with humanity, "perfectly re-established in Christ" (CCC 1042). The new heavens and the new earth will feature the heavenly Jerusalem, where God will dwell among the community of the redeemed. "The beatific vision, in which God opens himself in an inexhaustible way to the elect, will be the ever-flowing wellspring of happiness, peace, and mutual communion" (CCC 1045). The *Catechism*, quoting St. Irenaeus, describes the renewal of the visible universe, transformed "so that the world itself, restored to its original state, facing no further obstacles, should be at the service of the just," sharing the glorification of the living Christ (CCC 1047).

So why does God need to transform the world, and what will make it different from the present age? Two elements stand out. The first is God's actual presence in the new earth whereas He never resides in Eden or the existing (old) earth (CCC 1044). The second is that everyone admitted to Heaven has freely chosen to come and has demonstrated the ability to love completely and unconditionally either during their lives on earth or in Purgatory (CCC 1038). This sets the stage for a world perfectly ordered to God's will. This present earth is a period of testing, whereby we respond to God's invitation to Heaven with love. We demonstrate our true desires, not with words but with actions, when we build up love, Heaven's currency, and we are rewarded with joy.

The Church's teaching on the Last Day helps us understand God's plan better. First, we now understand why everything in this world is transitory, including our lives. This world was not built to last forever. We also begin to view evil and suffering from God's perspective. Evil is necessary for us to see and experience what life is like without God and His goodness. Suffering can drive us to seek a required good. Suffering creates different feelings to help us discern what the problem is. For instance, if we are hungry, we know we need food, whereas if we are lonely, we need companionship — the two feelings are distinct enough that anyone can tell the difference.

Sometimes God withholds His goodness, putting evil in our lives so that we can experience the alternative to life with Him, or to make it clear to us that this is not our permanent home. This can be why we experience the loss of material goods as physical evils. All material goods are finite. Christ and His Church preach that we should seek treasure in Heaven rather than treasure on earth, which will be lost when the world is renewed. As Jesus explains, "Where your treasure is, there also will your heart be" (Matt. 6:21).

The biggest question, of course, has always been what God wants from humanity. Jesus told us the answer to this question with the parable of the Prodigal Son, doing so in very clear terms that no one could miss if he or she makes the effort to read it: He wants us to be with Him. The story has a dynamic that we can all grasp. In the parable, the father shows the depths of his love, mercy, and forgiveness by running to his wayward son with open arms, not even mentioning that the son had taken half his property, left him, and then wasted his share of the estate.

As magnanimous as the father's love is in the parable of the Prodigal Son, it can never rival what God has done for us. In the parable, the father forgave the son who wasted his inheritance. In real life, God forgave the sinners who killed His Son, which is each one of us. In doing this, God has demonstrated His love and forgiveness.

The Christians of the first centuries were not exaggerating when they claimed that the world was created for the sake of the Church (CCC 60). They understood that God created the world for humanity in order to share Himself with us in love as a foretaste of Heaven.

It now becomes clear that the main reason the world exists is to populate the Kingdom of God with people who want to be there, with people who have learned to love divinely. This would explain why Jesus told the Sadducees that there was no marriage in Heaven (Matt. 22:23–33). If there was marriage and procreation in Heaven, then the people born in Heaven would not have had the opportunity to learn to love through suffering and to decide that self-giving love is what drives our ultimate happiness. Suffering allows us to learn the value and nature of the good. At the same time, it is the thought that sin begets evil, corrupting the good that comes from our union with God, that compels us not to sin.

Jesus is the ultimate judge of our lives, especially on the Last Day. We certainly choose how we live our lives. To reach Heaven, we will need God's help in a myriad of ways. We must also never forget that Jesus, the all-knowing and authoritative judge, is both infinitely just and infinitely merciful. That balance requires that Jesus gives all who choose to repent and follow Him access to Heaven, but it also requires their love and repentance, as we will see. If Jesus did not require these conditions, then the motivation for conversion would be greatly reduced, as would the purity of Heaven.

HEAVEN

Death is the doorway to God's Kingdom, where God waits for us with open arms. Death has no sting for the faithful Christian and is not to be feared. Death is also the end of our test on earth. This, in itself, is a sign of God's mercy and love because He lets us evaluate for ourselves whether we can live the life of love required in His Kingdom. He invites every soul to the wedding feast of Heaven. If we say yes to His invitation by getting baptized and we remain faithful to our baptismal promises, then we wait in joyful anticipation for God to call us home.

What makes Heaven joyous is the presence of God, the source of everything good, true, and beautiful in the universe. Those who, like the son in the parable, do not really know God, and therefore are not seeking to join with God, fear death. These people follow their instincts especially when it comes to preserving their lives and avoiding suffering. These instincts are good and useful to a point. The instinct to preserve our lives comes from God, and it encourages us to respect His sovereignty over life and death. Every person is given a finite amount of time to seek God's Kingdom. If we cut our time short by committing suicide, we are, in effect, choosing to separate ourselves from God. The instinct to avoid suffering is really a proxy for avoiding the evil (lack of good)[10] that suffering detects.

Jesus founded His Church to spread the good news about His defeat of death and to invite us to join Him in the Kingdom of God. Without access to the gospel message, we would be left with just our instinctual aversions to suffering and death to direct our actions. This is trying to carry out the most important task of our existence without getting the directions or knowing the goal. It is understandable that a person in this situation would be frustrated and angry, but to direct those feelings toward God, who has been trying to get our attention through suffering and the evangelization efforts of the Church and who has gifted all men with the internal law to guide them, is misguided, counterproductive, and wrong (Rom. 2:12–16).

Those who die in the state of grace, and who love so profoundly that they have no desire or tendency to sin, will be given immediate entrance into Heaven, where they will be in the presence of God, the

---

[10] John Paul II, apostolic letter *Salvifici Doloris* (On the Christian Meaning of Human Suffering) (February 11, 1984), no. 7.

angels, and the saints (CCC 1023, 1030).[11] Being one with God is to be united with all that is beautiful, good, and true in the universe. This Beatific Vision fulfills every need of mankind forever, providing pure happiness and joy (CCC 2548). Imagine a divine version of the Internet, which accesses the unlimited imagination of God and is filled with everything that is good, beautiful, and true, without the bandwidth and connectivity problems of the human Internet, and you will have a small sense of what will be there to share with the most loving and supportive people who ever existed.

PURGATORY

Those who die in the state of grace but are imperfectly purified, having not reached the level or intensity of love that would eliminate any unholiness (the desire or tendency to sin), will be assigned to Purgatory for final purification prior to entrance into Heaven (CCC 1030). Purgatory should be considered an extensive lobby or gateway to Heaven. Once in Purgatory, we are guaranteed entrance into Heaven at the completion of our cleansing (CCC 1030). We do not know how this works, but it can be assumed that our love will be strengthened through something analogous to the four tasks of suffering on earth. The existence of Purgatory is a great kindness from a merciful God because it reduces the requirements to get to Heaven during life, allowing for the final purgation of the tendency to sin after death.

---

[11] St. Thomas explains in *De Malo*, q. 7, art. 2, ad 9, 17: "Guilt is not remitted by punishment, but venial sin as to its guilt is remitted in Purgatory by virtue of grace, not only as existing in the habit, but also as proceeding to the act of charity in detestation of venial sin." This is described in the *Catechism* (1030): "After death they undergo purification, so as to achieve the holiness necessary to enter the joy of heaven." Further, as described in CCC 2013, all Christians are called to holiness, which is the perfection of charity, doing the will of the Father in everything.

Hell

Hell is reserved for those who have deliberately defied God through unrepented mortal sin (*CCC* 1033). Mortal sin is a serious offense against God, done with full knowledge and consent (*CCC* 1857). Said another way, this is actively defying or ignoring God, knowing that is what you are doing and the ramifications of that course of action. Think about that for a minute: not only do you have to offend God with a major offense, but you have to know that by carrying out the offense, you are going to Hell by your own choice, and you still have to be willing to do it.

This is, at best, disrespectful of God, but most would regard this type of behavior as hateful. There is no way that anyone would do that to someone they love. If you did this to your spouse, it would be very difficult to repair the relationship because most spouses would see this as an unforgivable, spiteful act. Not so with God, who is more merciful and forgiving than any human. God has no malice and is fully focused on where we are going, not where we have been. All God wants is for us to recognize our sins, to be sorry for them, to do penance, and to sincerely try to avoid them in the future. In other words, He is only concerned that our future actions are just because He loves us, and in His mercy, He is willing to forget past offenses, regardless of how offensive they were.

Unfortunately, those in Hell have rejected God's mercy, hating Him despite His love. The type of person who will end up in Hell may include those who thought that they had it easy in life, accumulating wealth and power with ease and limited suffering so that they feel that they do not need God or the help of others. They don't fear God or the evils in Hell. In fact, they may view the absence of God as a convenience, being glad that no one judges them in Hell or stops them from exploiting their neighbors. Of course, those in Hell have to contend with Satan and the demons in addition to their neighbors, so even the strongest, most evil man will be humbled in Hell.

CHAPTER 3

UNDERSTANDING LOVE AS
A PATH TO SALVATION

When Jesus was asked by the Pharisees to select the greatest commandment of the law, He responded with "You shall love the Lord, your God, with all your heart, with all your soul, and with all your mind. This is the greatest and the first commandment. The second is like it. You shall love your neighbor as yourself. The whole law and the prophets depend on these two commandments" (Matt. 22:37–40). Later, at the Last Supper, He told His disciples, "I give you a new commandment: love one another. As I have loved you, so you also should love one another. This is how all will know that you are my disciples, if you have love for one another" (John 13:34–35). Note, Jesus does not define what He means in words; He has physically shown them love from the beginning and will do so again with His Passion.

St. Paul also conveys this new commandment's power and importance without completely defining it:

> If I speak in human and angelic tongues but do not have love, I am a resounding gong or a clashing cymbal. And if I have the gift of prophecy and comprehend all mysteries and all knowledge; if I have all faith so as to move mountains but do not have love, I am nothing. If I give away everything I own, and if I hand my body over so that I may boast but do not have love, I gain nothing.

Love is patient, love is kind. It is not jealous, [love] is not pompous, it is not inflated, it is not rude, it does not seek its own interests, it is not quick-tempered, it does not brood over injury, it does not rejoice over wrongdoing but rejoices with the truth. It bears all things, believes all things, hopes all things, endures all things.

Love never fails. If there are prophecies, they will be brought to nothing; if tongues, they will cease; if knowledge, it will be brought to nothing. For we know partially, and we prophesy partially, but when the perfect comes, the partial will pass away. When I was a child, I used to talk as a child, think as a child, reason as a child; when I became a man, I put aside childish things. At present we see indistinctly, as in a mirror, but then face to face. At present I know partially; then I shall know fully, as I am fully known. So, faith, hope, love remain, these three; but the greatest of these is love. (1 Cor. 13:1–13)

In this hymn's first paragraph, St. Paul asserts that good works without love have no spiritual value, thus validating the concept that love is the eternal currency that gives meaning to everything. In the second paragraph, he defines love by the virtues that one possesses and the vices that one lacks, guiding us closer to imitating Jesus. In doing so, St. Paul reveals that love is an action, a decision of the will, rather than a feeling. In the third paragraph, St. Paul shows that love is the most valuable of the spiritual gifts because it is the only one that is eternal. Love also animates and gives form to everything. As a spiritual gift, love is from God and cannot be earned or purchased.

St. John, the "beloved apostle," clearly states that "God is love, and whoever remains in love remains in God and God in him" (1 John 4:16). Pope Benedict XVI opens his encyclical commenting on this verse: "These words from the First Letter of John express with remarkable clarity the heart of the Christian faith: the Christian image of God and the resulting image of mankind and its destiny."[12] By this Benedict means that we are destined to become like God, learning to love completely and unconditionally. We share in the divine nature, so that we can partake of God's life forever by knowing, loving, and serving Him, "man's last end," according to St. Thomas Aquinas. It is God's goal for humanity, in which man finds his true happiness.[13] To share in the divine nature is completely consistent with Jesus' teaching in the parable of the Prodigal Son, where the Father's goal is for His wayward children to freely come home to Him (Luke 15:11–32).

Although we cannot fully describe God's love, because it is beyond human expression, we can describe its actions and effects. St. Thomas uses this approach. He starts by defining love, but then quickly explains its actions and effects. He describes love as pertaining to the appetite because both love and appetite desire what is good. He recognizes that love is the principal movement toward the beloved regardless of the nature of the appetite,[14] and because the desire is generated by the object of the desire, it is defined as a passion.[15] Quoting St. Augustine, Thomas notes that love is defined to be the change in the appetite caused by the object, bringing them into union. The lover then moves toward the beloved, which he calls desire, and then rests united with the beloved, which results in joy.[16]

St. Thomas then studies the causes and effects of love. He notes that the cause of love is goodness because goodness denotes desirability, and love is the attraction to an external good. Thomas maintains that evil is never loved except under the aspect of goodness,

---

[12] Benedict XVI, encyclical letter *Deus Caritas Est* (God Is Love) (December 25, 2005), no. 1.

[13] *ST* I-II, q. 1, art. 1–8.

[14] *ST* I, q. 26, art. 1.

[15] *ST* I, q. 26, art. 2.

[16] *ST* I, q. 26, art. 2.

insofar that it is attached to some good. Thomas also finds that knowledge is a cause of love, because without knowledge of a thing, you cannot judge its goodness.[17]

The first effect of love is the union of the lover and the beloved, according to St. Thomas. This can be considered in two ways, the actual union where they share in each other's lives and the union of affection in which the bond is love itself.[18] He extends this concept to include the concept of mutual indwelling, in which the lover seeks to gain an intimate knowledge of the beloved, penetrating into his very soul.[19]

St. Thomas states that love causes zeal in the lover, in protection of the beloved. He also says it can cause ecstasies, which are defined as being out of oneself, explaining that the person experiences this by dwelling on and in the beloved. He denies that love wounds the lover, because he has already defined love as being adapted to the beloved, which is good for the lover and perfects him. He accepts that everything is done for love because everything is done for some reason. Love is the desire for some good, so he logically admits that everything is done for love of some kind.[20]

St. Thomas's insights on love are critical because they enable us to think about love in a comprehensive, cohesive way. We understand love's pervasiveness and its predominance because it is the principal movement toward any desired good. The physical senses desire material goods because they are associated with pleasure. This is why people say they love pizza, which is the love of concupiscence.

An appetite driven by reason also exists, resulting in rational love, of which friendship is a prominent example. Following Aristotle, St. Thomas defines friendships as relationships between people

[17] *ST* I, q. 27, art. 4.
[18] *ST* I, q. 28, art. 1.
[19] *ST* I, q. 28, art. 2.
[20] *ST* I-II, q. 28, art. 3–6.

with shared interests in things that are useful, delightful, or virtuous, benefiting both parties. When indulged in for pleasure or usefulness, friendship is self-serving, even though it is shared. Only when friendship is pursued for virtue does it become self-giving.[21]

There is also charity, which is a love associated with the appetite of the soul. Charity longs for union with God. St. Jerome says that charity, "true friendship cemented by Christ, is where men are drawn together, not by household interests, not by mere bodily presence, not by crafty and cajoling flattery, but by the fear of God, and the study of the Divine Scriptures."[22]

St. Augustine said, "Charity is a virtue which, when our affections are perfectly ordered, unites us to God, for by it, we love Him."[23] This statement deserves to be examined. By defining charity as a virtue, St. Augustine reiterates the notion that charity is a good habit — an action, not a feeling. Because charity is ordered to God, this virtue allows us to unite with God, and this union with God is love. The feeling we get from charity is called joy.[24]

When St. Paul spoke of love in his letter to the Corinthians, he was clearly talking about charity, using the closest Greek equivalent, *agape*. St. Thomas adds emphasis to what St. Paul said, calling charity the most excellent virtue, denying that any true virtue can exist without charity and insisting that charity is the form of all the virtues. Furthermore, St. Thomas justifies his previous point by declaring that charity is ordered to God and, hence, has the highest and best end possible, with all other ends being subservient to union with God, which results in man's last end, happiness.[25]

---

[21] *ST* II-II, q. 23, art. 1, resp. to obj. 3.
[22] *ST* II-II, q.23, art. 1
[23] *ST* II-II, q. 23, art. 3.
[24] *ST* II-II, q. 28, art. 1.
[25] *ST* II-II, q. 3, art. 1–8.

Both St. Thomas and the Catholic Church teach that charity is a gift from God that cannot be purchased or earned. God infuses charity within us according to His plan (CCC 1813). St. Thomas argues that charity is indeed a self-giving, voluntary human action, as opposed to God working through us. His view is that if God is working through us, then we would not be responsible for the action, and that would change the very nature of love as an act of the individual will.[26] Instead, in the infusion of charity, the Holy Spirit must enhance the person's appetite toward self-giving without interfering with his free will.

Sin, whether committed actively or committed passively by omission, represents a failure to love. Sin opposes God's will. In the parable of the Last Judgment (Matt. 25:31–46), Jesus shows us the consequences of our actions. Those who show love to the least of their brothers enter the Kingdom of God, while those who fail to love are left out in Hell. The Church calls this state a fall from grace, meaning you have separated yourself from God through sin and will no longer receive His graces, including infusions of charity. If you separate yourself from God in not loving others as you should, the only way we know of to reconcile with Him after Baptism is through sacramental Confession.

THE ORDER OF LOVE

Because every individual and situation are unique, no experience of love is the same. But is there an order to love — that is, are some people more worthy of being loved, and what makes them worthy? This important question can lead to a few responses. Everyone wants to be loved and, hence, searches for what makes them more lovable. At the same time, people want to know who they should love and why.

St. Thomas often pondered this question. Although his analysis is perhaps tainted by his life experiences as a thirteenth-century celibate

[26] *ST* I-II, q. 23, art. 2.

friar, his wisdom and insight deserve the utmost respect. St. Thomas adamantly believes that there is an order to love. He starts with a basic definition of love being the principal movement of an appetite to an external good.[27] The appetites of the higher faculties are given more importance than the lower ones. Hence charity, which is love ordered to God and an appetite of the soul, is the highest form of love. The love associated with the bodily senses, which Thomas calls the love of concupiscence, is the lowest form. This includes the love of material things, such as pizza, wine, and horses. Love that results from the human will is somewhere in between. This includes friendships, which are defined as relationships based on shared interests.

Charity is the most important love. St. Thomas even attempts to outline who we should love most according to charity. God is at the top of the list because He is the cause of happiness for which all humans strive.[28] In addition, God is the source of all charity, infusing in us the disposition to love Him directly and through the love of our neighbors, friends, and families. In fact, Jesus shows us that God identifies with the least of our brothers, saying, "Whatever you did for them, you did for me" (Matt. 25:40).

Keeping in mind that the role of charity is to bring us into union with God, St. Thomas reflects on how charity affects our relationships with our neighbors. St. Thomas teaches that in charity, man ought to love himself more than his neighbor because, in doing so, he has a full share in the divine good, which is more reason to love himself than being a partner in that share. St. Thomas gives us an insightful example of how this might work.[29] He points out that a person who loves himself more than his neighbor avoids sin to keep his neighbor from sinning, since reaching Heaven is the purpose of life.

[27] *ST* I-II, q. 25.
[28] *ST* I-II, q. 3, art. 8.
[29] *ST* II-II, q. 26, art. 4.

On the other hand, St. Thomas teaches that you should love your neighbor more than your own body.[30] St. Thomas says that charity does not require us to endanger our bodies for our neighbor's sake, unless we have an obligation to do so. However, if we choose to do so, he states that "it is perfecting charity."[31] What he is pointing out is that suffering and even dying for someone is redemptive, showing the highest form of love like our Savior on the Cross.

There is also value in reviewing St. Thomas's ordering of the "neighbors," because it gives insight into how God prioritizes loving relationships and how we should do the same. The deepest loving relationship is the spousal relationship. This is reflected in Scripture in several ways. St. Thomas takes special note of Jesus' answer to the Pharisees' question on divorce:[32]

> He said in reply, "Have you not read that from the beginning the Creator 'made them male and female' and said, 'For this reason a man shall leave his father and mother and be joined to his wife, and the two shall become one flesh'? So they are no longer two, but one flesh. Therefore, what God has joined together, no human being must separate." (Matt. 19:4–6)

Jesus' answer to the question of divorce encompasses the entire theology on marriage. Two complementary sexes (male and female) exist for the purpose of procreation. This is made physically possible when the two become one flesh, but this also defines the new family unit that occurs when the spouses leave their parents to set up a new household. Finally, God has joined the couple with bonds of love, which no human should separate. These bonds are divine. No person has ever been able to make someone else fall in love with them or was able to

---

[30] *ST* II-II, q. 26, art. 5.
[31] *ST* II-II, q. 26, art. 5, resp. to obj. 3.
[32] *ST* II-II, q. 26, art. 11.

fall in love with someone of their choosing. Humans, however, have free will and can refuse to marry their true love. You can ignore the "spark" from God, but you cannot create it. The choice to ignore it, however, comes at a price, for the couple themselves, who will suffer heartaches and always wonder what might have been, and for onlookers that see their pain and can become worried that their own partner will reject them and become noncommittal themselves.

This construct has some significant ramifications about how a person makes him- or herself more lovable. People of faith know that the more closely they follow God, the more lovable they will be to other people of faith, and also to God, whom they trust to put them in a situation that is best for them, whether with a marriage partner or not. At times, God chooses for some people to serve Him in some capacity by remaining single. Other times, it is the person's selfishness that keeps them and their potential partner single. Sometimes God gives people a second or even a third chance at love if they lose their partner to selfishness or even to death.

Modern society has different priorities, emphasizing physical attractiveness, which ironically drives people toward "physical enhancements" to make them look like the societal ideal. This takes away the person's natural perfection for the role God planned for them, separating them from Him and His infusion of charity. It does appeal to lust and attraction, which are poor substitutes for love, but for those who do not trust in God, it is natural for them to trust in themselves or medical science, albeit with far inferior results.

Beyond spousal love, St. Thomas summarizes relationships in the following way: "A thing is loved more in two ways: first because it has the character of a more excellent good, secondly by reason of a closer connection."[33] While this definition works for adult relationships, St. Thomas failed to appreciate the innate bonding of a mother

[33] *ST* II-II, q. 26, art. 12.

with her preborn child and the bonding of parents with their children in general. Specifically, because St. Thomas believed that the soul and all the genetics were transmitted from the father, and that the mother served only as an incubator, his theology placed the love of the father ahead of the love of the mother.[34] If St. Thomas had access to modern biology, which proves that each parent donates half the child's genetics, he would likely have switched the order of love to mother over father, which is consistent with modern expectations and experience.

St. Thomas does not clearly identify whether it is proper to love your parents or children more. He notes that a man is more united to his children than his father but that the father is likely closer to God. It obviously depends on the situation and the people involved.[35] Because virtue makes a difference in the lovability of a person, St. Thomas agrees with St. Ambrose that "good servants should be preferred to wicked children."[36] This is probably true for adult children but is less certain for young children who are being trained by their parents. Parents generally are bonded to their children in a way that makes them strong advocates for their offspring against all criticism — plus, being responsible for a child's education, they have a vested interest. It seems unlikely that a parent would prefer a good servant to a younger child who is wicked, because they will be able to see the child's potential in which they have a role to play and will explain their faults away as part of a work in progress.

Beyond the nuclear family, which God protects with specific bonds of love because of its importance as the building block of all society (CCC 2207), St. Thomas teaches that a person is more lovable by becoming a better person — aligning oneself more closely

---

[34] ST II-II, q. 26, art. 10.
[35] ST II-II, q. 26, art. 8–11.
[36] ST II-II, q. 26, art. 8.

with God or being connected more closely with the beloved.[37] To act in complete charity, a person must put the other's needs before his own, thus sacrificing for the good of the other. This would meet both requirements, making the person the most lovable they can be by loving in the best possible way.

St. Basil wrote about the correct motivation for charity, which is to act as children of God:

> If we turn away from evil out of fear of punishment, we are in the position of slaves. If we pursue the enticement of wages,... we resemble mercenaries. Finally if we obey for the sake of the good itself and out of love for him who commands, we are in the position of children. (*CCC* 1828)

God loves us in a variety of ways, starting with our existence and everything we are and everything we have. To experience His love in the fullest possible way, we must use the fruits of His love — our skills, desires, resources, and opportunities — to love Him back, which will be demonstrated by showing charity to those He loves and otherwise doing His will. The more we use our love, the more intense it becomes.

This is also a use-it-or-lose-it situation. If we fail to pass on God's love to others, we will lose the ability to love, which is to fall from God's grace. This fall from grace is usually discussed as being the result of a mortal sin, but it can be equally well described as a lack of love. Indeed, when we sin, we are acting counter to Jesus' will. This may be a sin of commission, if we act counter to His will deliberately, substantively, and with full knowledge of the ramifications of our actions.[38] This is clearly counter to love, and no one who truly loves would act in this way toward his beloved. It can also be a sin of

---

[37] *ST* II-II, q. 26, art. 12.

[38] These "limitations" on mortal sin separate sin from accidents, which are unintentional, and mistakes, which are due to a lack of knowledge. They limit sin to fault on the part of the sinner.

omission if we fail to alleviate another's suffering when we have the opportunity. If either happens, we will need to reconcile with God sacramentally, to return to the state of grace and get back the ability and motivation to be charitable.

CHAPTER 4

SHARING GOD'S LOVE

To reach Heaven, we must share God's love with those we meet. The Greeks provide us with a time-tested baseline that has been embedded in their language from antiquity. It is said that the Greeks had six different terms for love.[39] Actually, this is not true. What is true is that they identified at least seven types of loving relationships, without defining love at all. This is exactly what we need for this study of love, for the Greeks' wisdom on loving relationships still applies for our times.

In the Septuagint, the Church-recognized Greek translation of the Old Testament, and the New Testament, which was written mostly in Greek, only three of the Greek words were chosen to describe love. *Eros* (romantic love) is used twice in the Old Testament and never in the New Testament. *Philia* (brotherly love or the love of friendship) is used to describe Jesus and His relationship with His disciples, and *agape* (charity) is used to describe our relationship with the Father and with our neighbors.[40] Four other types of relationships will be considered for completeness.

---

[39] Roman Krznaric, "The Ancient Greeks' 6 Words for Love (and Why Knowing Them Can Change Your Life)," *YES! Magazine*, December 28, 2013, https://www.yesmagazine.org/health-happiness/2013/12/28/the-ancient-greeks-6-words-for-love-and-why-knowing-them-can-change-your-life.

[40] Benedict XVI, *Deus Caritas Est*, no. 3.

PHILAUTIA: PROPER SELF-LOVE

This is perhaps the most misunderstood type of love, particularly in today's secular society. Most people would agree that to love oneself is to take steps that will lead to happiness. But what leads us to happiness, and is it the same for everyone? This question has been taken up by the greatest philosophers of all time, among them Aristotle, St. Augustine, and St. Thomas Aquinas. St. Thomas synthesizes the views of St. Augustine, who lived eight hundred years before him, and Aristotle, who lived seven hundred years before that, in his *Summa Theologica*, which itself was written eight hundred years ago. He finds all three are in agreement that happiness is the goal of man (man's last end) and that true happiness results from the greatest good of man.[41]

If happiness is the goal of man's existence, the question then shifts into a new one: What is the greatest good that makes one happy? Many today deny that there is a singular greatest good for all men; instead, they believe that goodness is relative to the circumstances present in a given situation. St. Thomas believed that God is the greatest good, being the source of all that is. And it is in the Beatific Vision that man experiences the most profound happiness, fulfilling his every desire.[42] Even the pagan Aristotle, while having no understanding of the Beatific Vision, recognized that "it is reasonable that happiness is God-given ... [but] even if it is not God sent but comes to be present through virtue and a certain learning or practice, it is among the most divine things."[43]

Many view self-indulgence, consuming lavishly and doing anything one pleases, as the greatest good that makes one happy. Others view proper self-love as living a healthy lifestyle, one free of stress

---

[41] *ST* I-II, q. 1.

[42] *ST* I-II, q. 2, art. 8.

[43] Aristotle, *Nicomachean Ethics*, trans. Robert C. Bartlett and Susan D. Collins (Chicago: University of Chicago Press, 2011), bk. 1, chap. 9.

and filled with exercise, nutrition, and plenty of sleep. St. Thomas addresses both as goods for the body, which are temporary and thus inferior to goods of the soul. Furthermore, since self-indulgence and a healthy lifestyle are not the greatest good, they cannot be the ultimate source of happiness.[44]

Similarly, St. Thomas addresses all of the traditional earthly goals valued by secular society — wealth, power, fame, honor, glory, pleasure, and material goods — and finds all of them deficient in being the ultimate source of happiness because they all are temporary and limited in some way.[45]

Proper self-love looks very different for those who know and love God than it does for people who do not, because they have different mindsets. The believer looks to Heaven for fulfillment while the nonbeliever looks to this passing life. Do we not recognize that all our material possessions will be left behind when we die? Therefore, proper self-love goes beyond taking care of our physical bodies. It means we are looking out for our best way to happiness. If we truly love ourselves, we will love God, who made us and is calling us back to Himself through His Church. At the same time, we will seek to embrace our sufferings, learning from them our path to salvation. At the same time, we will seek to avoid inflicting suffering on others by our own sins.

Self-love requires that we understand our fundamental relationship to God — we are His children, made perfectly for His plan. There will always be someone who excels at something better than we do. That's to be expected, and it is part of our discernment process. When we find ourselves deficient in a role even when we do our best, then that is not the role God planned for us, and we should keep searching for a match. It is, after all, God's plan and He wants it to succeed, so He makes sure

[44] *ST* I-II, q. 2, art. 5, 6.
[45] *ST* I-II, q. 2.

that everyone has what they need to fulfill their role or roles, and He uses suffering to let us know if we are in the wrong role for us.

Most people have multiple roles to carry out in life, and our most important roles (coach, mentor, teacher, parent, friend, child, sibling) are normally not the ones from which we earn a living. These roles come naturally to us if they are part of God's plan, and carrying them out will be easy because we were made for them. Further, God presents them to us in a way that we will be successful if we follow His direction. The way to discern if you are in the right role is by seeing if you can act with love in this role, avoiding and/or alleviating suffering, and if you are energized by carrying it out. In short, you will feel joy in doing what you were meant to do. If you are trying to carry out a role that was meant for someone else, you will not enjoy it and will soon become frustrated because either you will feel underutilized or you will find you cannot adequately handle the role with your skills, experiences, and resources.

In some extreme cases, people get confused about their very identities because strong forces label them in ways that, although harmful, are repeated with such frequency that the person starts to believe the labels and begins to do what others expect. This includes telling children that their gender identities are fluid and that, with hard work, anything is possible. Many people feel that this is giving freedom of choice to individuals and being open-minded and supportive about how others feel about themselves. In reality, and regardless of the person's intentions, these statements are actually lies, and by untethering the recipients from the truth, they are disabling. We all need to be grounded in the truth to know how to act. If everyone has their own version of the truth, then there is nothing real that can be counted on. This would render living impossible, because to make valid plans, you must have a stable base to project the outcome.

These lies distract people from discerning their true role in God's plan. Instead of finding roles that match their skills and interests and allowing them to love their neighbors, society drives the young toward roles in which they can build up material wealth, power, and prestige, while simultaneously causing them to doubt what is really true about themselves and the world around them. Indeed, in the last homily he gave before becoming Pope Benedict XVI, Cardinal Joseph Ratzinger warned, "We are building a dictatorship of relativism that does not recognize anything as definitive and whose ultimate goal consists solely of one's own ego and desires"[46]

Living a false identity does not breed peace and comfort, and certainly not joy. Instead, it causes inner turmoil, driving many to take up coping mechanisms like drugs or alcohol that end up causing even more harm. God will use suffering to motivate them back to their true identity as His children. And through His Church, He can help them overcome the evil lies that have enslaved them.

In the end, proper self-love must lead to happiness, which is union with God. This requires storing up riches in Heaven, rather than on earth. It further means that proper love of self begins with the love of God, which ought to spill over to our neighbors. It may seem paradoxical to modern sensibilities, but true happiness comes not from accumulating and using material wealth but from giving of oneself for the common good, creating bonds with those whom we love. By doing so, we are building love, Heaven's currency. This will end with eternal joy in the presence of God. To use our lives to prepare ourselves for entering God's Kingdom is the best possible kind of self-love.

LUDUS: PLAYFUL, FLIRTATIOUS LOVE

To flirt is to seek commitment from another without offering any commitment of our own. It is not a loving relationship per se because it is noncommittal while seeking out a commitment from another.

---

[46] Joseph Ratzinger, homily at the Mass *Pro Eligendo Romano Pontifice* (April 18, 2005).

Love without reciprocation is a tragedy and causes one of the deepest forms of suffering. It is so painful that many are very hesitant to admit their feelings to their loved ones for fear of being rejected. Flirtation mitigates the fear of rejection. It is an immature love because it seeks commitment without offering any in return. In the best cases, once their partner commits to them, the flirtatious individual will also commit to a loving relationship, which we call *eros*. Sadly, some people flirt for the sake of manipulating those around them. They can then leverage the other's feelings to get sex, money, or power.

We do not have to flirt with God because He always makes the first move in our relationship, lovingly creating us and sustaining us at every moment with His grace. In fact, as mentioned in chapter 1, if we align ourselves with God's will, we will see the wisdom of God's plan and we will cease to be afraid of being abandoned by Him.

PHILIA: DEEP SELF-GIVING FRIENDSHIP

Philia describes how groups of people love one another deeply but not romantically. *Philia* differs from *eros* in that *filial* relationships are not sexual, while *erotic* relationships are meant to be procreative. People are attracted to one another as friends when they share a common good. Attraction differs from love in that attraction is one-sided, coming from the mind and the body's senses. Friendship can progress to love if God infuses the parties with the desire and opportunity for spiritual bonding.

In reality, filial bonds greatly outnumber erotic bonds because most moral people have only one erotic partner (their spouse) at a time but may have many people to whom they feel bonding but not romantic ties. Filial bonds typically involve groups of people tied to a cause they all believe in or from shared experiences; such connections are marked by the willingness of their individual members to sacrifice for the good of the others. This type of love is also used to describe men who fight together in battle, trusting each other with their lives. In the New Testament, it is used to describe the apostles' relationship with Jesus and the other disciples. It also refers to a sibling's love (of either sex) but could include any group of friends, of either sex, as long as they desire to work together on a common interest, sacrificing for the good of others. St. Thomas Aquinas, writing mostly for his celibate peers, discusses love in terms of *philia* rather than *eros*. *Philia* shares a special bond, which distinguishes it both from *eros* and mere friendship. Indeed, friendly goodwill is strictly a reasoned judgment, while love is a passion, which St. Thomas describes as an "eager inclination."[47]

Filial bonds are natural with true siblings because we share the same relatives and grow up together. Yet there can often be resentments associated with real or perceived injustices that siblings may harbor. The resulting estrangements demonstrate a lack of love and can only be resolved if the aggrieved party takes the initiative, shows their vulnerability, and is willing to forgive the oppressor.

Filial bonds extend beyond natural siblings to anyone you love platonically. It can be a college roommate, high school friends, work associates, or members of clubs or associations. Ideally, we would look at every other human as worthy of filial love.

Eros: Romantic Love

Romantic love between a man and a woman is the most obvious type of love because it is experienced by everyone, directly or indirectly. After all, God created two complementary sexes to facilitate our existence and, except in very rare cases, assigned every person to be male or female as part of His universal design and plan for salvation.[48]

---

[47] *ST* I-II, q. 27, art. 2.

[48] A small number (0.018 percent) of people are not readily classified as male or female biologically (defined as intersex). Leonard Sax, "How Common Is Intersex? A Response to Anne Fausto-Sterling," *Journal of Sex Research* 39, no. 3 (2002): 174–178, https://doi.org/10.1080/00224490209552139.

It also seems certain that God is a divine matchmaker. To the consternation of many, humans really have no control over who they fall in love with or who falls in love with them. You cannot make someone fall in love with you, nor can you fall in love with whoever you choose. Many believe that love is unpredictable and "just happens." People discuss this as having chemistry or a spark with another. What they are experiencing is actually an infusion of love by God that spiritually bonds the lover and the beloved.

Eros is clearly part of God's plan and was meant to be consummated in the matrimonial covenant until death. *Eros* is ordered toward the good of the spouses and the procreation and education of the offspring (CCC 1601). The *Catechism of the Catholic Church* offers some beautiful reflections on this topic: "The intimate community of life and love which constitutes the married state has been established by the Creator and endowed by Him with its own laws" (CCC 1603). "The well-being of the individual person and of both human and Christian society is closely bound up with the healthy state of conjugal and family life" (CCC 1603). And finally, "God who created man out of love also calls him to love — the fundamental and innate vocation of every human being. For man is created in the image and likeness of God who is himself love. Since God created him man and woman, their mutual love becomes an image of the absolute and unfailing love with which God loves man" (CCC 1604).

Eros or romantic love is often confused with lust or physical attraction. Lust seeks to use another person for sexual gratification. Lust distorts real love and is not from God. Attraction is when we want to be with the other person because they do or represent things that we admire. Attraction alone is not love; love must be acted on. Neither are all actions love; self-centered actions are not love. Love must be driven by the desire implanted in our hearts by God, the ultimate matchmaker, to give ourselves to another.

Without the infusion of love from God, which is often described as chemistry or a spark, only friendship remains. While friendship is good, it can never sustain both marital love and raising children because it lacks the bonding that love provides. Mutual self-giving love and God's sacramental graces are necessary for a marriage to endure and produce joy.

People who experience attraction to another person, but who have never been in love, wonder whether it is the real thing. If you have to wonder, it is not the real thing. When God brings a man and a woman together, He makes the bond so clear that even onlookers can see that there is something more than attraction. Once God has led you to your future spouse, it is your responsibility to follow His plan and experience the joy associated with love. If you fail to heed the call of love, you will regret it, as will your chosen partner. In fact, the suffering associated with lost love is so extreme that some people are afraid to admit their love to their partner for fear that their love will not be returned or that the love is not real. If neither partner is ready to take the first step, then the marriage cannot happen, which is a tragedy for both partners.

For those called to marriage, finding one's spouse is one of the most important tasks in life. We can distinguish love from lust and physical attraction by assessing whether the relationship is aligned with God's plans for us. If a married man tells another woman (not his wife) he loves her, he is not professing true love because adultery is a sin. Rather, he is expressing his lust or attraction, which is driven by human thoughts and desires. She should not return his love, even if she feels attracted to him, because it will lead to sin and unhappiness for all involved.

Similarly, same-sex attraction should not be mistaken for *eros* because God's Word declares homosexual acts to be immoral at least three times and they are naturally unfruitful.[49] God would not

---

[49] Lev. 18:22; Rom. 1:26–27; 1 Cor. 6:9.

contradict Himself by infusing *eros* into same-sex couples. Same-sex attraction and an attraction itself differs from love in that it is a product of the human intellect, and as such, the attraction is toward something that the admired person does or represents.

Many same-sex-attracted individuals wish for their relationships and their love to be recognized as equal to heterosexual marriage. The truth says otherwise. Same-sex partners lack the complementary genitals required to have intercourse, and therefore, they can never create new life together. Marriage equality is impossible for same-sex couples to achieve in reality because it goes against God's design stamped into their very bodies. Still, the same-sex advocates use clever terms, such as "marriage equality" and "love is love, "to twist the truth, hurting both the people involved and society.

God has not abandoned those with same-sex attraction, nor has He denied them the opportunity to love. The love they experience may be *philia* rather than *eros*. As discussed previously, *philia* and *eros* are both forms of love that God initiates. *Philia* drives humans toward spiritual bonding, not sex or reproduction. In both *philia* and *eros* cases, God infuses His love into the lovers and follows up with whatever is needed to tighten the bond between them. The response of the person to the person he or she is bonded with is a measure of the love and respect that he gives to God and His plan and to his or her partner. The intensity of this person's love will grow the more he loves. It will diminish in both purity and intensity if he fails to respond to love with love.

Eros involves the mutual self-giving of the partners and is meant to be fruitful, producing children in marriage. *Eros* reaches its full potential in the sacrament of Matrimony, through which God's grace enables a couple to "help one another to attain holiness in their married life and in welcoming and educating their children" (CCC 1641).

As strong a force as *eros* is, it cannot take away man's free will. Even when God brings two people together, they must both freely give their consent for a marriage to be valid (CCC 1626). Once validly married, they still must will the best for their spouse, or their love will be lost. Many say that marriage is hard work, and it can be, if they face life's challenges as individuals and not as a couple. But as long as both spouses remember that, of all the potential partners in the world, God gave them this one to love and to care for above all others, then marriage is not only easy but joyous. Marriage not only allows souls to fulfill God's plan but also helps them to overcome self-absorption, egoism, and the pursuit of one's own pleasure. Ultimately, marriage leads to heroic self-giving love (CCC 1609). St. Paul concluded that husbands must give authority over their own bodies to their wives and wives give authority over their bodies to their husbands. This is not only in a sexual sense, but in everything they do for one another.

The joy of falling in love and getting married to the right person cannot be overstated; the greatest poets and writers have not done it justice. Some couples describe it as this sense of completeness, marking their complementariness, while others say they are at home with each other wherever they are. Further, the joy of a good marriage is obvious to even casual observers. This joy will carry over to other relationships as well, since a good marriage will make both partners better people. It is a preview of God's Kingdom, where everyone will love each other fully and unconditionally because they are God's children. To reach Heaven together, both spouses must work on their holiness together.

Matrimony is a sacrament of service to conceive, bear, and raise children to become members of God's Kingdom. Not everyone, however, is called to this type of service. Some are called to serve God through Holy Orders or consecrating their lives to God. Others have roles in God's plan to show and grow their love in different ways that are more appropriate for people who are free of the marriage vocation.

STORGE: LOVE BETWEEN PARENTS AND CHILDREN

In God's design, children are the fruits of a married couple's love. It is a direct demonstration of the growth of love as two become three. Just as God gave the spouses each other to care for, God also gives them children to love and care for. Becoming a parent changes our lives profoundly. When parents first hold a newborn child in their arms, it is hard not to be struck by the immense responsibility that God has entrusted them with in raising this child to be a happy, productive member of society and, more importantly, the Church. The parents naturally see themselves and their spouses in their children, so they are motivated to help them succeed, but the best of parents also see God in their children, so they are motivated to sacrifice to aid in God's plan rather than being motivated by the self-centered thought of carrying on their legacy through their children. They understand that God gave them this child to raise to help bring forth His Kingdom. This is also true of an adopted child who shares no direct lineage with the parents. In any case, parenthood is an act of charity, with the parents sacrificing for the good of the children.

The relationship between parents and children teaches us how God loves us. It is love in its purest form on earth, with most parents loving their children unconditionally, even though it causes the parents to sacrifice. In fact, raising children always results in some sacrifice from the parents, whether it is losing sleep to comfort a crying infant or the use of parental resources to feed, clothe, and educate their children to adulthood and sometimes beyond. Because parental love is, by nature, self-sacrificial love, being a parent leads most people to be the best versions of themselves. Despite the sacrifices, most parents enjoy being with their children, watching and aiding in their growth. Parenting is extraordinary training for the Kingdom of God. Heaven is populated with souls that care for everyone, as if each soul were their own child.

At the same time, those who enter God's Kingdom look upon God as well-cared-for children look upon their parents. Young children are completely dependent on their parents and want nothing more than to cuddle with them. This is a child's first experience of joy, a joy that the parent shares. Children feel safe with their parents, especially when they sustain an injury. Parents can stop their children's crying by kissing their wound. Well-raised and well-loved children often idolize their parents, telling everyone who will listen that they want to be just like their parents when they grow up.

When children reach puberty and become more independent, they no longer cling to their parents. This transition is natural and good. It can also result in hard feelings if the parent won't allow healthy separation or if the teen abuses his new freedoms.

When God blesses a couple with a child, the parents must still choose to love that child, because love is an act of the will. If the parents are inattentive or — worse — abusive, their love will die. Love needs to be exercised in any relationship if it is to become stronger.

Parents can normally be counted on to defend their children in all circumstances. And yet sometimes parents do not stand up for a child, leaving the child feeling abandoned and no longer loved. It takes a lot for children to turn against their parents and for parents to turn on their children. It is a personal and community-wide tragedy when parents forsake a child because someone must now raise him.

It is, on the other hand, a great blessing to a community when people extend parental love to children who are not their own. The best teachers, coaches, tutors, foster parents, babysitters, and mentors treat all their charges like they would their own children. In good neighborhoods, all the parents look out for all the children. It does not take a community to raise a child, but it sure is nice when they help out in loving the children.

PRAGMA: SETTLED LOVE IN LONG-STANDING RELATIONSHIPS

Pragma is the love experienced by older couples who have raised their children to adulthood and who no longer have, or need, the hormonal stimulus to love as in the *eros* and *storge* periods of their relationship. Now it is love for love's sake. Couples who reach this stage have typically been married for more than half their lives and have so many shared bonds and experiences to draw from that they have truly become one. This stage is idyllic, as each spouse joyfully serves the other, which is on display for all to see.

But with old age comes degeneration, which is a harsh reality for *pragma* to overcome. Inevitably, one partner will get seriously ill and will not be able to fulfill his or her customary roles in the marriage. This puts strain on the other partner, who might now be forced to take on many unfamiliar responsibilities. Ultimately, one partner may have to become the caretaker for the other. Not only does this change the relationship dramatically, but it also signals an end to the relationship through death. This can be the source of great sadness and even anger, both at the spouse for abandoning the survivor and at God for taking the spouse. But in the countless cases that I am aware of, long-term love (*pragma*) is strong enough to withstand even this.

This is certainly the case in my marriage, where my wife, Sue, takes me on daily walks to keep up my strength and plays a board game with me every night to keep my mind sharp. She has silently picked up the chores of mowing the lawn and taking out the trash while at the same time holding me accountable for the things I can do, like picking up after myself. She is often a better judge of what I can and cannot do than I am, and she will force me to "use it or lose it."

Pragma is mature love, and it also is part of God's plan. Love does not end with death; it is Heaven's currency, transcending death. When an older couple attends to each other's needs and does it because of their vows before God and their love for one another, their self-sacrificial love can become redemptive. The sick spouse is willing to be the one ill so that his or her spouse can be well and can gain the spiritual merit of self-sacrifice while being the caregiver. The dying spouse should do everything possible to help the surviving spouse prosper when he or she is left behind. They should get in the habit of praying for each other so they can continue to be connected by prayer when the first one dies. A good marriage is when both spouses help each other reach Heaven so they can be reunited after death. God wants this too, so He smiles on couples who have stayed faithful to each other and to Him until the end.

That said, it is not a betrayal of the marriage vows if the surviving spouse remarries. In fact, God may be rewarding the surviving spouse with companionship and comfort for taking their original spouse from them. The prior spouse's death serves for someone's salvation. Jesus explicitly taught that there is no marriage in Heaven (Matt. 22:30). Indeed, the two most important functions of marriage, to conceive and raise children and to help each other to get into Heaven, must be completed on earth, and so there is no need for marriage in Heaven. Furthermore, everyone in Heaven loves God and loves as He loves, so there is no jealousy surrounding one's former spouse's actions. The spouse in Heaven will be happy if their former spouse on earth is happy.

AGAPE: EMPATHETIC LOVE OF OTHERS

Agape (*caritas* in Latin, *charity* in English) is the term used by the New Testament authors to describe the type of love that one has for others simply because they are children of God. "Charity is the theological virtue by which we love God above all things for His own sake, and our neighbor as ourselves for the love of God" (CCC 1822). It is the type of love that God has for us and that we are called to share with others. It is giving of ourselves without expecting anything in return.

> The practice of all the virtues is animated and inspired by charity, which "binds everything together in perfect harmony"; it is the *form of the virtues*; it articulates and orders them among themselves; it is the source and the goal of their Christian practice. Charity upholds and purifies our human ability to love, and raises it to the supernatural perfection of divine love. (CCC 1827)

It is divine love, out of the reach of fallen man, who is only motivated by what benefits him directly and immediately. It can only be practiced fully by the grace of God and for God and the successful completion of His plan. It is the currency of Heaven, and it elevates men to share in the divine nature.

St. Thomas recognizes love as the principal *action* associated with charity. Charity is then defined as man's friendship with God, the kind of deep friendship that extends to all that are connected to God.[50] Furthermore, every friendship is based on a shared good. St. Thomas concludes, "The friendship of charity is based on the fellowship of happiness, which consists essentially in God, as the First Principle, whence it flows to all who are capable of happiness. Therefore, God ought to be loved chiefly and before all out of charity: for He is loved as the cause of happiness."[51]

St. Thomas states that "charity increases by being intensified in its subject, and this is for charity to increase in its essence; and not by charity being added to charity."[52] "This is what God does when He increases charity, that is, He makes it to have a greater hold on the soul, and the likeness of the Holy Spirit to be more perfectly participated by

---

[50] *ST* I-II, q. 23, art. 1, resp. to obj. 2.
[51] *ST* I-II, q. 2, art. 1.
[52] *ST* I-II, q. 24, art. 5.

the soul."[53] St. Thomas also adds that "charity does not actually increase through every act of charity, but each act of charity disposes to an increase of charity, in so far as one act of charity makes man more ready to act again according to charity, and this readiness increasing, man breaks out into an act of more fervent love, and strives to advance in charity, and then his charity increases actually."[54]

Said differently, love is not a commodity that can be accumulated like money in a bank. Love is different. Love is a capability that is grown and refined with use and practice. Love behaves like muscles or the human mind. With use, it grows in both strength and tone. Conversely, without constant use, it withers and dies. Because love is united through the soul to the infinite God, it can always be increased in purity or intensity as long as we live.

St. Thomas, along with the Church, holds that charity is infused into man by the Holy Spirit (CCC 1813). St. Thomas argues effectively that charity cannot be God working through us directly because that would eliminate the freedom that true love requires — it must be self-giving, so it can never be forced on someone and be love. Instead, St. Thomas says God gives us the capability to love and adds that "it is most necessary that, for us to perform the act of charity, there should be in us some habitual form superadded to the natural power, inclining that power to the act of charity, and causing it to act with ease and pleasure."[55]

As St. Thomas says above, love is the principal action of charity, but it is more than just an action. Charity must also include a disposition, a way to think, which is entirely focused on another person you will give yourself to. Charity bonds you to those you love. It is a deep desire placed in your soul of divine, not human, origin. This disposition to

---

[53] *ST* I-II, q. 24, art. 5, resp. to obj. 3.
[54] *ST* I-II, q. 24., art. 6.
[55] *ST* I-II, q. 23., art. 2.

seek the best for the ones you love, and the desire to be with them, is seen in the fulfillment of every one of the Beatitudes and in every type of loving relationship we experience.

While the disposition to charity or any form of love comes from God, love always remains an act of the will. As St. Thomas explained above, it would not be love if we did not will it and take action. In addition, love doesn't rise to the level of charity, which is to love divinely, if it is not self-giving with the intensity that can lead to your willingness to suffer for the other's benefit.

When most people today hear the word *charity*, they think of individuals or even corporations donating goods or services to those in need. Used in this sense, a charity is an organization that acts as a conduit between charitable givers and the recipients. But this usage does not fully reflect the concept of theological charity. Charity of divine origin must be in support of God and His plan. Jesus explained that those who give alms in order to be seen by others will get no recompense from God because "they have received their reward" (Matt: 6:1–2). Even worse, some groups call themselves charities while opposing Christ and His Church's teachings. These generate not charity but righteous condemnation.

CHAPTER 5

RECOGNIZING GOD'S LOVE

Some people find God's love only after extreme duress. For these individuals, God is literally breaking them down to save them. In many cases, it seems like those who suffer the most are being prepared for bigger roles in God's plan. St. Thérèse of Lisieux marveled that "God showered extraordinary favors on saints that offended him; for instance, St. Augustine and St. Paul, whom he forced, so to speak, to accept His graces."[56] She pondered why God favored some from cradle to grave while allowing "poor savages to die in great number without even hearing the name of God pronounced."[57]

Jesus taught St. Thérèse this mystery through the book of nature. She came to understand that "all the flowers he created are beautiful. How the splendor of the rose and the whiteness of the lily do not take away the perfume of the little violet or the delightful simplicity of the daisy."[58] She realized that if "all the flowers wanted to be roses, nature would lose her springtime beauty and the fields would no longer be decked out with little wildflowers."[59] And so she makes the connection that "the world of souls is Jesus'

---

[56] Thérèse Martin, *Story of a Soul: The Autobiography of St. Thérèse of Lisieux*, trans. John Clarke, O.C.D., 3rd ed. (Washington, DC: ICS Publications, 1996), 13–14.

[57] Ibid., 14.

[58] Ibid.

[59] Ibid.

Garden. He willed to create great souls comparable to roses and lilies, but he created smaller ones, and these must be content to be daisies or violets destined to give joy to God's glances as He looks down at His feet. Perfection consists in doing His will, in being what He wills us to be."[60]

She further reflects that God must reach down lower for the child and the savage than for the Doctors of the Church, and in doing so, God manifests His infinite grandeur. She concludes that "just as the sun shines simultaneously on the tall cedars and on each little flower as though it were alone on the earth, Our Lord is occupied particularly with each soul as though there were no others like it. And just as in nature all the seasons are arranged in such a way as to make the humblest daisy bloom on a set day, in the same way, everything works out the good of each soul."[61]

When St. Thérèse died at the age of twenty-four, she had a very deep relationship with God. She was relatively uneducated from an academic point of view, but as we have seen, she understood and could explain the intricacies of God's love in a way that most children can comprehend. She inherently grasped that God makes each one of us perfect for our given roles, and He will make everything right in the end because of His great love. She also trusted God, even when He took her mother away when Thérèse was four years old.[62] From an early age, she could see the big picture that God was elevating her mother into Heaven, not penalizing those who survived. Indeed, the Church validated her confidence in this regard, canonizing both of her parents.[63]

---

[60] Ibid.

[61] Ibid., 14–15.

[62] Ibid., 33, 34.

[63] Fr. Carl Markelz, O.Carm., "Humble Servants: The Canonization of Louis and Zélie Martin," Society of the Little Flower, October 19, 2015, https://www.littleflower. org/carmelites/humble-servants-the-canonization-of-louis-and-zelie-martin/.

As insightful as St. Thérèse is, her humility kept her small. She saw herself as a little flower, but God raised her to the same status as those she defined as "roses and lilies." She was declared a saint in 1925 and declared a Doctor of the Church by John Paul II in 1997. She has spent her Heaven helping souls on earth, just as she desired.[64] God answers the prayers of those aligned with His will, often in unexpected ways.

As St. Thérèse points out, things are not always as they seem, and God has a plan in which everything works out for both the daisies and the roses. Ironically, the first step to understanding God's love for us is to look at the times we have suffered most because that is when we have been helped the most in our path to salvation. These suffering events are the critical points in our lives that define us. Suffering detects when we lack or lose critical goods that threaten not only our lives but our existence. When we look back at these episodes of suffering, it is important to take the time to contemplate what lessons were being taught to us by our loving God. We need to remember, as we do so, that God is far less concerned with things that we gain or do not gain on earth than He is about helping us come home to Him as faithful members of His Church and, ultimately, His Kingdom. If we look at suffering only from a material, earthly perspective and disregard the spiritual growth it leads to, then we are counting the cost while disregarding the gain, which is infinitely more valuable. Our perspective on this can change how we feel from disillusion and discouragement to joy.

Like suffering and death, love is a universal phenomenon that few people truly understand. Like suffering and death, love comes at seemingly unpredictable times to people who are not expecting it and have done nothing to deserve it. Love and suffering are very much intertwined, with suffering identifying where love is missing

---

[64] Martin, *Story of a Soul*, 263.

while the loss of love brings about much suffering. Said another way, suffering is an "evil detector," and evil is a lack of love, so suffering also detects when we are not loved or have not loved. To be complete, love is an action that alleviates suffering because it alleviates the evil that suffering detects. While everyone's life is different, there are some common themes that will highlight the interaction between suffering and love that will show how a loving God uses earthly suffering to direct us away from evil and toward eternal life.

At the beginning of our spiritual journey, suffering indicates those areas that keep us from loving God, ourselves, and each other. For instance, if you are prone to excessive drinking, you will suffer from a hangover, which is God's message to you that you are hurting yourself as well as providing motivation to stop. If you are not eating well, you will feel unwell, which should lead you to attempt to eat healthier. Every bad habit results in suffering that will not dissipate until the person either changes these vices into virtues or dies. God is persistent in His call for us.

God allows suffering to make it abundantly clear what is good for us and what is not. Without suffering, people can easily make decisions hazardous to both body and soul. Since God made everything good for its desired purpose, all evils have some associated good that appeals to some people. As discussed earlier, evil is the deprivation of good, and people will logically choose evil if the good associated with the evil is more desirable than the good of which the evil deprives us. For instance, the medical community has warned people for years that smoking causes cancer and reduces a person's overall health and expected lifespan. Yet people continue to smoke for various reasons that trump any negative health side effects.

Another way to look at suffering is that the evil it detects can be separated into two categories: the evil of punishment and the evil of fault. Punishment is called evil because it technically takes some good away from the guilty, but it is a community good because it provides a deterrent to the evil of fault. Fault, on the other hand, includes all the disordered choices people make, choosing lesser goods over greater goods, which is unjust and the basis of all sin. There is no fault with God, because He is perfect, and so only the evil of fault is immoral, in conflict with providence, God's great plan for the salvation of man.

Some people find fault in punishment, claiming that punishment of any kind is not demonstrating love, and may suggest that positive reinforcement is the loving way to bring about good behavior. But this is an argument over nuance. In such a system, something without positive reinforcement, or even with less positive reinforcement, would be the new punishment. This view is also naïve because it fails to recognize that nothing is completely evil and that various attributes associated with evil can lead people to commit the most heinous crimes.

If people are not disciplined, they will have difficulty recognizing right from wrong, and they can harm themselves and others physically, spiritually, emotionally, or psychologically. Consider the parents that you know. The attributes of a good parent include being active in the child's development, explaining and demonstrating the rules of good conduct, and disciplining the child when their behavior is harmful, rather than loving, to others or themselves. Unloving parents think only of their own needs, and by being largely absent to their children — or worse yet, abusive — they teach their children to also be self-centered.

Punishment that is meant to build up goodness, like God practices, takes effort and thought, which is why it is different from most human punishments, which are merely punitive. Therefore, the more you suffer on earth, the more God is conforming you to Himself and the more love He is giving you. Understanding this point leads one to joy, whereas if we dwell only on the discomfort of suffering, we may fall into despair.

Many people object to those who do evil and are seemingly not punished, while those who never seem to suffer count themselves as blessed. These people, who never consider the spiritual parts of their being or notice their lack of spiritual growth or the harm they cause others by either malice or indifference, may come to think of themselves as not needing God, turning away His help and guidance, and will find themselves outside the Kingdom when they die. They are not to be envied but rather pitied and mourned.

Any action that is counter to love will cause suffering to the perpetrator, either directly or indirectly. It causes suffering indirectly when your loveless actions negatively affect another person and they share their suffering with you, either through complaints or retribution. This too is the action of a loving God, who is training us to see that when we act in love, suffering is avoided or mitigated, but it increases when we stray from the path to His Kingdom.

Sometimes we are called to suffer for others, just as Jesus Himself did. We might suffer for a loved one because we don't want them to struggle. This is mourning their condition, which, as we know from the Beatitudes, is an expression of love. It might also be that someone is oppressing us and our role is to correct the sinner by suffering in a nonjudgmental, loving manner. Hence, God is giving us the opportunity to heroically witness through suffering and thus carry out His plan while building up heavenly currency. This redemptive love to forgive and love our persecutors rather than to seek retribution for our loss is the perfection of love.

Some people wish to escape their sufferings by chasing after fame, fortune, and power. In doing so, they neglect everything else in their lives, including God and even their spouse, children, relatives, and friends. In His great love, God may mercifully disengage the person from his or her temptations in several ways. For instance, if a person is totally focused on making money, God might humble him through financial ruin. The person will then need to rely on the charity of others which will allow him to see the relative merits of eternal love versus material goods. While others caught up in the same drive for material wealth will see this as a huge catastrophe, the person directly affected will hopefully see it for the mercy it is, if not in this world then perhaps in the next one. The problem is that few people realize that suffering is our greatest teacher, for it makes us stronger and more like Christ if we heed His lessons.

God also makes His presence and His will known through suffering. We can appreciate God's wisdom, His will, and His great love for us in two ways. One way is to observe what causes and what alleviates suffering — and to recognize that this is aligning oneself to God's will (to become prudent). For those not motivated enough to consider these things and to recognize that they are a sign of God's love, then God may visit them with an evil that cannot be ignored and can be resolved only by God. This may come in the form of a disease or some other type of suffering that changes their entire perspective of the world. In the case of St. Paul, he had to be thrown from his horse on the road to Damascus and blinded in order for him to see the light of Christ (Acts 9:1–9). There are many other saints that have undergone life-changing sufferings. For example, both St. Ignatius Loyola and St. Francis of Assisi were converted during long convalescences that followed battlefield injury or illness.[65]

Sometimes God's plan requires that we suffer in order to bring others to the Faith. Indeed, eleven of the twelve apostles named by Jesus died martyrs' deaths to demonstrate the depth of their faith and love of God. St. Paul said that he received thirty-nine lashes five times from the Jews, had been beaten with rods three times, once was stoned, and three times was shipwrecked (2 Cor. 11:24–25).

---

[65] Sr. Rosemary Stets, O.S.F., "The Conversion of St. Francis of Assisi," Franciscan Media, November 17, 2022, https://www.franciscanmedia. org/franciscan-spirit-blog/the-conversion-of-st-francis-of-assisi/.

God works mostly through secondary sources to bring us to Himself. He puts certain people into our lives in different ways to alleviate our suffering, teach us to love, and serve as our companions. God works through His Church, which is why it is called the Body of Christ, but He also can use even nonbelievers to conduct His work.

It is important also to recognize those who have shown us love in our lifetimes. Everyone is capable of giving and receiving love from others, but true love always originates with God. When people love us, it is prompted by God, but it is of their own free will that they act on it. Not everyone does, for if love is not freely given and there is no choice to deny love, then it is not love that we are talking about. It is more like exploitation, where we are forced to give ourselves to others.

God loved us first, even before we came into being. He conceived us in His mind before our mothers did, placing us with the right parents at the appropriate time and place, with all the skills and attributes necessary to accomplish His will. Sometimes the parents we are given are inattentive or, worse, abusive. In these situations, God can use children to help save their parents, by teaching them to love. In the rare case where the parent fails to love their children, some onlooker may eventually intercede for the children, whether it is a family member or child protection services.

Sometimes God gives us difficult parents to prepare us for greater work. Dan Burke, who started the Avila Institute for Spiritual Formation, had a very harrowing childhood that prepared him for his future ministry in spiritual warfare. Burke describes his childhood as a constant emotional tornado that some of his siblings did not escape alive. He explains that most of his surviving siblings have been in and out of drug rehab, have attempted suicide, and lead generally destructive patterns of life.[66] In one childhood story, Dan describes

---

[66] Dan Burke, *Spiritual Warfare and the Discernment of Spirits* (Manchester, NH: Sophia Institute Press, 2019), 3.

facing the terror of his parents having a full-volume and frightening argument, then a gunshot, followed by an eerie silence that left nine-year-old Dan and his two brothers huddled in the basement wondering if their mother was dead or if they were next.[67]

Unlike his siblings, Dan Burke found God and the teachings of the Catholic Church or, perhaps better, God found Dan. God used Dan's childhood sufferings and experiences to build a ministry that continues to positively affect countless lives through several platforms, including his books, his shows on EWTN, and most of all the Avila Institute, which trains spiritual directors from around the world.

God "handcrafts" each person — we are all unique individuals — to carry out particular roles in society and in the Church. He also puts people in our orbits at the right time and place to provide the things we lack. It can be just a few words to redirect us toward what God needs from us and them. It may be that a person can play a significant role in our lives without understanding that they did anything out of the ordinary. God knows what everyone will do in a given situation, and He has the foresight and power to modify the situation to get the results He wants.

Six particular instances of this come to mind in my own experience. When I was a forty-year-old cultural Catholic, God called an unknown priest to give me the penance of attending a weekday Mass. At the time, I thought it was an uncomfortable inconvenience I did not deserve, but it changed my whole perspective on doing something for God above the minimum. I have no idea who that priest was or why he gave me that penance, so I doubt whether he knows how life-changing it was.

About ten years later, I encountered Sr. Marie Pappas when she became the director of religious education (DRE) at St. Columba Parish in Hopewell Junction, New York, where I had been a catechist

---

[67] Ibid., 4.

since the time of my reversion. Sr. Marie, who was overqualified for her role, encouraged me to expand my horizons beyond the parish, preparing me to respond to the dream I had to "teach the teachers," which propelled this entire ministry of suffering.

The third person who had a great effect on my life was the first neurologist I saw in Virginia, after I was diagnosed with Parkinson's and had already committed myself to the move and the change of careers. Upon learning that I was getting a doctorate in theology at Catholic University, my doctor asked me why people have to suffer. I replied that I didn't have a clue since it was not my field of study. She then convinced me that it was a more worthy topic than the one I intended to study. The university allowed me to transfer to moral theology under the direction of Dr. Paul Scherz, who just happened to be the instructor in the first class in which I tested my suffering thesis. He validated that it was a subject worth pursuing and offered to direct my studies, which was providential. He offered great advice while being exceptionally available and responsive, which was exactly what I needed at that time. Less than five years later, I earned my doctorate, and the first book in this series, *Why All People Suffer*, was published.

Even after publishing my first book, God placed other people in my path at critical junctures. The next person who produced a very profound effect on my journey was John Halligan, the most talented member of the first department I ever managed at IBM. I admit to being challenged by his excellence, so rather than build him up as I should have, I mismanaged him, causing him to seek refuge with another manager. Almost thirty years later, I discovered what a good man John truly was. After I posted my suffering book on LinkedIn (not sure how John saw it), he was the first person to reshare my post.

Amazed at his kindness, I thanked him profusely and sent him an electronic copy of the book before it was published. John then helped me set up a website, which he had experience with because he had been working on his own suffering ministry, the details of which I was only slightly aware of prior to this encounter. I knew that he had a son who committed suicide and that he had subsequently quit IBM. What I did not know was the intensity of his love for his son, Ryan, and all who would suffer like Ryan, including those who bullied his son mercilessly, causing him to take his own life. I learned the details in his excellent book, *Ryan's Story*.

On my journey, I have been blessed to meet people who have experienced God's great love and kindness even under terrible stress. Sometimes it is obvious to them, and sometimes it is a bit more elusive. Certainly, John Halligan is one of those for whom understanding God's love for him came later. After all, his son Ryan was an early victim of cyberbullying, tragically committing suicide at the age of thirteen. John's reaction to the searing emotional pain was to try to prevent as many people as possible from sharing that pain by leading a personal crusade against cyberbullying. John has told Ryan's story to more than one million middle school students in school assemblies over the last twenty years. Even more impressive, John showed true love to the two students most responsible for Ryan's death, which allowed them to repent and be forgiven.

John's book, *Ryan's Story: A Father's Hard-Earned Lessons about Cyberbullying and Suicide*, does a tremendous job of showing the pain he felt at the loss of his son. It is beyond commendable that John was able to master his own emotions and try to make sense of his son's suicide while every week he recounted it to parents and students and psychologically relived the story. Much of the book describes John's search for what he could have done to prevent his son's death, just as the title suggests. For many years John was filled with self-pity and assumed that he was experiencing God's wrath. Only after he realized that God used his suffering and that of his son to reduce future suffering for others, and that this kind of love was redemptive, did he begin to heal emotionally and spiritually. He now saw himself as an instrument of God's love, charged with protecting other youths from cyberbullying. Having returned to his Catholic roots, especially the sacrament of Reconciliation, he felt immense relief and peace for the first time in almost twenty years. Love never fails, as St. Paul described, even in the worst situations. That is because God *is* love and is all-powerful. When you align with God, you will always succeed because God never fails.

I met Garrett Johnson when he was a student of mine at the Avila Institute of Spiritual Formation. I knew very little about him since it was an online class and we have never met in person. One day he asked me whether I would read *his* book. I was admittedly unprepared for the darkness and intensity of his story and the graphic way he presented it. I was also impressed with the honesty and intelligence with which Garrett wrote.

Garrett's powerful story has a multitude of lessons embedded within it. His descent into darkness destroys many of the paradigms that are spoken of as truths in modern society, and his reemergence into the light seems nothing short of miraculous. Yet, God reaches out to everyone, even the most fallen who have chosen to embrace darkness and addiction.

Garrett's book begins with him being taunted as a six-year-old with the words "You are gay." Garrett didn't understand what that meant at the time, and he was certainly not sexualized at age six, but the taunting persisted throughout his childhood and into adolescence from many different sources.[68] It happened so often that Garrett began to believe it — and to think the easiest path forward was to embrace the title. At one point in his youth, a girl he had a crush on convinced him to put on a wig and a dress. He mistook her laughter for approval and walked home in this attire, making his father angry.

---

[68] Garrett Johnson, "Becoming a Good Man" (unpublished book manuscript, 2023), 1.

Garrett had a good relationship with his father in his early life, but as he got close to his teens, tension developed, and their relationship soured because Garrett was so undisciplined. Garrett's father did not have the tools to bring him under control, resulting from his own difficult upbringing. Out of frustration, his father pushed many of those he loved away, including Garrett. Garrett learned from his father's behavior that the way to deal with people who hurt you is to hurt them back. This hurting included leveraging his mother's love to hurt his parents' relationship. Once, when they were playfully wrestling, he purposely kneed his father in the groin. This opened the rift with his father even more, as you might expect. After this split, Garrett saw only the worst in his father, seeing every act of love as somehow an example of his father's self-centeredness, and he took every opportunity to harm his father. As his relationship with his dad continued to deteriorate, he grew closer to his mom, who seemed to reflect his tender, kind side.[69] He began to see himself as more like a woman than a man.

During and after high school, Garrett's relationship with his father became untenable, and soon after graduation, Garrett enrolled in and then dropped out of community college. He found that it was too late to get his father's money refunded. He reenrolled to give it another shot, but he dropped out again, this time fully aware that he was wasting his parents' money. He deliberately did not tell his father until it was too late to get a refund. His father said he would no longer pay Garrett's tuition and gave his son an ultimatum: find a career or move out. Garrett followed the example of his older brother, who also left at eighteen when faced with the same decision. While Garrett's parents wanted him to grow up, they failed to realize that school was a hostile environment for him because of his classmates' taunts, which negatively impacted his ability to perform in college.

[69]   Ibid., 11.

His parents were also inconsistent in putting rules and structures in place for him to learn virtue and avoid vice. For instance, after they found a *Playboy* magazine he had in his possession, his mother and babysitter told him that the human body was good and his urges were natural.[70] Garrett knew that what he was doing with pornographic material was far from natural, and he commented in retrospect that the two most important women in his life approved of his sinful behavior rather than giving him appropriate limits. After leaving his parents' home, it seemed as though nothing would curb his excesses.

Having no real parental supervision, Garrett predictably ended up with a group of "friends" that hastened his plunge into darkness. He worked part-time at low-level jobs and lived in a room he rented in a house that was full of bad examples and a far cry from the upper-middle-class home he was used to. He hung out with his co-workers after work and began to drink heavily. He was underage, but one of his employers, no doubt thinking he was doing them a favor, would buy alcohol for Garrett and his friends. Garrett and his friends were labeled losers by society; they also had no ambition or inhibitions. Garrett, highly in need of attention and positive feedback, became more and more immersed in the gay lifestyle, frequenting gay clubs where "everyone knew his name." He had a few sexual encounters but found gay sex "gross" and "unsavory," and he also worried about contracting AIDS.

Something deep inside him, his Christian roots, made his forays into the gay lifestyle an internal conflict, and he developed a series of addictions as coping mechanisms. He continued to get drunk almost every day but slowly supplanted this with smoking marijuana. The two intoxicants served to blunt the internal conflict. He attempted to escape the darkness of his life through fantasy, which for him meant extensive gaming, pornography, masturbation, and shopping for high-end clothes, which he could not afford.

[70]   Ibid., 16.

These coping mechanisms simply added to his problems. To keep up this lifestyle, Garrett thought nothing of stealing from his employers and accepting money from a young woman who practiced witchcraft. The descent into darkness continued as Garrett and his "crew" vandalized their neighbors' property, even setting a fire that was so large it gained local media attention.

They valued their lives so little and had so little regard for others that they would drive the wrong way down twisting back roads with their headlights turned off. All these evil acts had no consequences because they were not caught, much to Garrett's surprise. Deep down, he knew his behavior was wrong. He felt that his authority figures were doing him a disservice by letting him get away with doing evil uninhibited, while they probably thought they were giving him a break.

With time, God started reaching out to Garrett in subtle ways that he did not recognize. One day at the salon Garrett worked at as a high-end hair stylist, a seemingly random customer was vigorously complaining about her father.[71] This brought out a defense of the customer's father from Garrett that he had no trouble recognizing as applicable in his own father's case as well. Garrett realized that his father had also received a poor upbringing and was doing the best he could in a difficult situation. This was the first in a series of blessings that allowed Garrett to reconcile with his family and eventually allowed him to see his path from darkness to light.

Around this time, Garrett's parents moved from Maryland to up-state New York. This transition led to many unexpected blessings. It increased his parents' marital harmony because Garrett's mother didn't want to move but knew her husband needed a change, especially for his own mental health. Garrett's father saw this for what it was, a sacrifice of love, and it went a long way toward mending the relationship

---

[71] Ibid., 89.

that the younger Garrett tried to sabotage. The distance improved Garrett's relationship with his parents as well. Garrett was no longer able to drop over without real commitment: the six-hour drive prolonged his stays. This helped Garrett begin to wean himself off pot because he didn't smoke as much while he was with his parents.

Spending extended time with his parents, away from his "friends," allowed him to see his mother and father as people and not caricatures. It also meant that when they argued, Garrett could no longer flee the situation but had to face it. Garrett and his father realized that they both were responding to verbal and nonverbal cues (the tone of his father's voice, for example) instead of listening to each other. Once they became aware of these signals, both tried to mitigate their effects and saw each other in a more positive light.

Garrett's mother was becoming an increasingly faithful Catholic and would share her thoughts with Garrett, although he was still resistant to the Church (but not to Jesus). His father also began to send him mail that Garrett now realized was to give him direction and support.[72] One day, while Garrett was telling his father on the phone about helping someone, his father uttered the words that Garrett had been longing to hear his whole life: "You are a good man."[73] It is significant that his father was able to show Garrett some love after all Garrett had put him through. It shows how strong and resilient love is, particularly parental love, and that we should never give up on those relationships, no matter what the situation is. It also shows how God can use our loved ones to deliver the messages we need to hear.

Garrett's father repeated these words frequently, and they began to sink in. Over time, Garrett began to realize that the labels that had been part of his persona were starting to melt away. Garrett started to

---

[72]   Ibid., 88.
[73]   Ibid., 95.

view himself as masculine, but the transition was rocky because he had so many labels to jettison. He had been called gay, a pothead, a loser, and a gaming addict. As he gained confidence and the acceptance of both his older brother and his father, he began to realize that none of those labels needed to be true. He began to see himself as God sees him, and as a result he recognized a new, better role for himself. Whereas before he used his persuasive power to lead people to the gay lifestyle, alcohol, weed, and gaming, he would now tell people about the God who saved him. He saw this as a way to help them avoid the labeling that caused him such pain in his life and the addictions he used to cope with it.[74]

God had put a puppy, named Lenny, in Garrett's life because Garrett was isolated and lonely. To the extent that he could at the time, Garrett loved the puppy, but he also neglected and abused Lenny. After years of mistreatment, Lenny got cancer and had two surgeries.[75] During Lenny's recovery from the surgeries, a different part of Garrett emerged: the tender, compassionate, gentle side of him that had been stifled when he was younger. This emergence brought pain to Garrett but also a desire to return to the person he used to be rather than the one he had become — a man so filled with hate, apathy, and selfishness that he couldn't be bothered to care for his own dog. Garrett was devastated by Lenny's death, perhaps in part because it showed his own mortality and unhappiness.

During this same time, Garrett started actively looking for ways to stop smoking marijuana. He began by making one day a week smoke-free. He attended a Marijuana Anonymous meeting but quit because a step in the twelve-step program said that he had to acknowledge that marijuana controlled him. He refused to accept this removal of personal responsibility and set off to quit cold turkey on

[74]   Ibid., 103.
[75]   Ibid., 101–109.

his own.[76] Importantly, he had begun to feel and work better when he was sober. This was also a time of recognizing that God did exist and that His plan for Garrett likely did not include getting high, playing video games, and looking at porn while living in a dingy basement apartment at age thirty-eight.[77]

As he smoked less, he began to see his priorities more clearly. He had more time for personal contact and began speaking to the neighbors, whom he had mostly ignored in the past. Finally, he was ready to quit smoking weed, so he asked God to help him stop, promising that if He did, Garrett would do whatever He wanted him to do with the rest of his life.[78] He went to stay with his parents for a week and, by God's grace, never smoked weed again after having smoked nonstop for at least ten to fifteen years.

Shortly after Garrett quit, his godmother, his best friend from childhood, and Lenny all died within a two-year period. These deaths made him reflect on how lonely and isolated he was.[79] He begrudgingly recognized and accepted that God did not create him to be alone, so he began to interact more with his family, started attending Mass on a regular basis, and set about assisting the poor and elderly.

His awareness of Jesus' personal love grew rapidly, and he decided to be confirmed in the Catholic Church.[80] During this process, he learned more about the Church's teaching on same-sex attraction and was introduced through his spiritual director to the Courage apostolate. Through Courage, Garrett experienced something he rarely had before: close male friends who were focused on growing in their relationship with Jesus and His Church and living chastely. He also began to see a Catholic therapist, who helped him reestablish

---

[76]   Ibid., 82.
[77]   Ibid., 75.
[78]   Ibid., 81.
[79]   Ibid., 127–128.
[80]   Ibid., 143, 150.

healthy relationships with all of his family members. These two factors transformed Garrett from a son of the world into a son of God who wanted nothing more than to grow ever closer to Christ and His Body, the Church.[81] Seeing that many people could not find spiritual directors, Garrett enrolled in the Avila Institute for Spiritual Formation to fill that void. It was there that I first encountered him.

Garrett has now been off marijuana for more than twelve years and has been a member of Courage, pursuing chastity, for ten years. He uses his free time to work to build up the Kingdom of God and to help free others from the lies that kept him trapped in a false identity, through his YouTube channel (youtube.com/@brotherwithoutorder), website (brotherwithoutorder.com), and unpublished autobiography, "Becoming a Good Man."[82]

God put John and Garrett in my life to help me see two types of suffering that I fortunately have not experienced. Both men's stories are redemptive, born from incredible darkness, with God giving them the grace and strength to help others avoid the suffering they endured. I am better for having known these two men. It is also a reminder that we can learn to love from others' examples without having to experience everything ourselves.

Love can alleviate or sometimes even help us avoid certain sufferings, but not necessarily all at once or instantaneously. As in Garrett's case, if there are multiple issues, it can take a while to work through them all. Nevertheless, as dark as that situation was, God's love prevailed when Garrett turned to Him for help. I hope someone will publish "Becoming a Good Man," because it is a powerfully provocative story of the redemptive strength of love in the harshest circumstances I have ever read about.

[81] Ibid., 150, 159.
[82] Ibid., 160.

God is active in all our lives, in most cases working through others. In retrospect, it is easy for most people to recognize those who have helped them in pivotal points in their lives, although they may not recognize God's role in the situations. This is because, as in my own case, the people placed in our paths to help us are undoubtedly God's instruments. You can be sure that my neurologist did not ask all her patients why people suffer. Perhaps one of her patients presented her with that same question earlier in the day, and encountering a person who was studying theology provided her with the potential to give that patient an answer. Regardless, that question changed my life's trajectory. By changing the environment, God creates the situation He knows will bring out desired results from us, without affecting our free will and often without us recognizing it.

CHAPTER 6

RESPONDING TO
GOD'S LOVE

I<small>F WE LOOK TO</small> our suffering to see the points in our lives that God most loved us, then we can point to the happiest days of our lives to see when we have come the closest to doing God's will, which is synonymous with acting in charity. In a recent poll, the top four events that made adults happy were the birth of a child, falling in love, getting married, and making meaningful friendships.[83] All four of these, of course, are classic examples of human relationships that are part of God's plan for us. People love God by loving those individuals He puts in their path, whether a spouse, a child, a friend, or a stranger who needs help, thus cooperating with God's will. A very small minority (less than 5 percent) chose events that are not based on human relationships but are related to achieving material goals, including graduating from school, getting a job, retiring from a job, taking a desired trip, buying a home, or gaining financial independence.

These results are not that surprising. Our supreme happiness is union with God, which was not mentioned in the poll. And yet does not God's love permeate the happiest moments of our lives, even if it is not recognized by those surveyed? Consider also that many of the materially related choices, like graduating from school or getting a

---

[83] "Happiest I've Ever Been: Exploring the Moments People Felt Happiest in Life," Happy Cards, https://happycards.com/blog/happiest-ive-ever-been/. What people view as the happiest events in their lives, of course, differs with age and circumstances.

job, are in line with God's plans for people. Excelling in school and work aligns with God's will for them. No one is happy when they are unsuited for their jobs or if their studies don't mesh with their skills and interests.

The more we are conformed with God's plan for us, the happier we will be, and that means showing love to everyone. Spiritual growth is rewarded with the feeling of joy. Now, some people think that pleasure and joy are synonyms. But I doubt that a person who thinks this has ever experienced true joy. Pleasure is a bodily sensation that lasts only as long as the body is in contact with a desirable object, like eating ice cream. Joy is a sensation of the soul. Unlike pleasure, joy can coincide with suffering and is indeed the positive outcome of suffering well embraced. It is the sweet feeling one gets when achieving a hard-won goal. Joy is experienced in life's most glorious events, such as the birth of a child after an intense labor. The joy of one's wedding day is the culmination of a long journey to find one's spouse, particularly for older brides and grooms. The same goes for falling in love and even entering meaningful relationships. Students experience joy upon successfully completing their studies and getting a job that fits their role in God's plan.

It is natural that joy and happiness follow suffering. Things that are rare and hard to achieve are valued more highly than common items that are easy to get, precisely because they are difficult. Gold is valued more highly than iron, not because of its utility but because it is rarer and harder to get. Devout souls can look back at their worst times of suffering and see God's hand, highlighting changes needed through their suffering. When they heeded the message of their suffering and made those changes to align themselves with God's will, they found joy or at least mitigated their suffering.

There is no true joy without struggle. Joy is a measure of spiritual progress, and progress takes effort. Why is that? Because things that are easy to do or easy to get are not valued highly and are often taken for granted. If we are following God's plan for us, then our path is typically straight and simple, devoid of suffering, and if we should stray from the path, God will provide suffering to direct us back in line. That said, this isn't always the case. Sometimes, in His wisdom, God's plan calls for the righteous to suffer for the benefit of someone's salvation. As discussed earlier, this was the case for Job in the Old Testament and St. Paul in the New Testament, who suffered tremendous hardships willingly in order to save other souls, thus saving their own.

But there is an easier way to learn God's will than to test and see what causes us to suffer. This is a last check. God sent Jesus, His only-begotten Son, to show us the way to Heaven. In the Gospels, Jesus gave us the new commandment of love (John 15:17) and at least three ways to fulfill it. He began the Sermon on the Mount, His great summation of moral theology, with the Beatitudes, a list of eight attributes that describe the divine nature (Matt. 5:1–12). To the rich young man who asked Him directly, "What good must I do to gain eternal life?" He answered, "Keep the commandments" (Matt. 19:16–17). In the final parable He told before His Crucifixion, Jesus explained the criteria that will be used at the Last Judgment, which involve administering the works of mercy to the least of His brothers (Matt. 25:31–46).

We will examine each of these three great lists (the Ten Commandments, the Beatitudes, and the corporal and spiritual works of mercy) in detail in the next three chapters. These lists are complementary ways to show us how to love. The Ten Commandments, given by God to Moses one thousand years before Christ (Exod. 20:1–17), define right and wrong and are the written form of the natural law, which is imprinted on the heart of every person (CCC 2070). The Beatitudes describe love in terms of attitudes that will lead to ultimate happiness. And finally, the works of mercy elaborate on the Ten Commandments, explaining different actions to help others, body and soul.

Recognizing God's love in our lives is important for our mental, physical, and spiritual well-being. It puts suffering in the right perspective and gives us hope for eternal life in place of the despair felt by those who do not recognize God's love. We also know from our earthly relationships that unreturned love soon dies. This is not the case with God, who loves us infinitely. If we cease to love God, we will lose the ability to love others, because all love begins with an infusion from Him. We will soon fall from grace without access to the sacraments. And when this occurs, we will find ourselves shut off from God's Kingdom if we do not reconcile with Him through His Church.

Returning God's love is essential to our eternal souls. If we want to live like God and be with God, we must love Him and all that He loves. At the Last Supper, Jesus described this way of love as the "new commandment" (John 13:34). Jesus also said that we show our love for Him by how we treat our suffering brothers and sisters (Matt. 25:31–46). When we love others, we are showing our love for God and, in the process, increasing our capability to love.

CHAPTER 7

THE TEN COMMANDMENTS

FOLLOWING THE TEN COMMANDMENTS has been the preferred way to Heaven since God gave them to Moses on Mt. Sinai thousands of years ago. Even Christ Himself, when speaking with the rich young man, acknowledged that the Ten Commandments were the way to gain eternal life (Matt. 19:16–26). These laws appeal especially to those who desire discrete direction. In fact, the rich young man asked the question that was on every thinking person's mind: "What good must I do to gain eternal life?" (Matt. 19:16). Jesus answered him, "If you wish to enter into life, keep the commandments" (Matt. 19:17). Indeed, the Ten Commandments provide the moral underpinnings for all the Church's teachings and the actions and teachings of Christ (CCC 2064). They define what is understood as righteous in the Beatitudes and are a written expression of the natural law (CCC 2080).

Noting that the Jews of His time were following the letter of the law, rather than its spirit, Jesus expanded on the fifth commandment (from killing to hatred), the sixth commandment (from adultery to divorce and lust), and the eighth commandment (from not making false oaths to taking none at all) (Matt. 5:17–37). Following Jesus' lead, the Church expanded all of them to clearly delineate the scope of each commandment so as to reduce the ambiguity and to express them in both positive (you must respect life from beginning to end) and negative (thou shall not kill) terms. The Church has conveniently laid out all her work on the commandments for the last two thousand years in *The Catechism of the Catholic Church* paragraphs 2084–2557. I have pulled out the highlights below, but you are, of course, encouraged to engage with the unedited version published by the Church.

If you find that you have been violating any of the Ten Commandments, God is calling you to repentance and conversion. This will be easier if you contemplate what is wrong with your action and why it offends God. If you are Catholic or Orthodox, seek out the sacrament of Reconciliation to cleanse your soul of mortal sin. God's mercy awaits you.

LOVE GOD (COMMANDMENTS 1–3)

The first three commandments are about loving God. These are the most important commandments as testified by Christ, who, in response to the Pharisee's question about the greatest commandment, answered, "You shall love the Lord, your God, with all your heart, with all your soul, and with all your mind. This is the greatest and the first commandment. The second is like it: You shall love your neighbor as yourself" (Matt. 22:36–39).

"The first commandment requires us to nourish and protect our faith with prudence and vigilance, and to reject everything that is opposed to it" (*CCC 2088*). We should turn to God and the Church to understand these parameters. St. John told Jesus that the apostles had tried to stop someone from driving out demons in His name because he did not belong to their group (Mark 9:38). Jesus responded, "Do not prevent him. There is no one who performs a mighty deed in my name who can at the same time speak ill of me. For whoever is not against us is for us" (Mark 9:39–40). The Church herself quotes St. Paul, who shows "'ignorance of God' is the principal and explanation of all moral deviations" (*CCC 2087*). The Church understands that "all men are called to this catholic unity of the People of God.... And to it, in different ways, belong or are ordered: the Catholic faithful, others who believe in Christ, and finally all mankind, called by God's grace to salvation" (*CCC* 836).

The search for God is a search for the truth. Those who search for God, whether Christians, Muslims, Jews, or adherents of other non-Christian religions, are far closer to Catholics than are the irreligious, who do not recognize someone greater than themselves who holds them accountable for their actions and is the source of all that is true. "The Church considers all goodness and truth found in these religions as 'a preparation for the Gospel and given by him who enlightens all men that they may at length have life'" (*CCC* 843).

What does all of this mean? It means that to be religious is to search for God, who is the Creator of all there is and hence the Creator of truth. In time, if you search for the truth, you will find Christ and His Church, for she possesses the fullness of truth. When leading others to the Church, ask the Holy Spirit to enlighten your mind and answer questions the best that you can. This is an act of love for your neighbor and for God as you appeal to reason. Trying to force religion on another, particularly through violence and threats, causes suffering and is evil, which is contrary to love.

"The first commandment is also concerned with sins against hope, namely, despair and presumption" (*CCC* 2091). Despair means that man ceases to hope for his salvation from God, while presumption means that man believes he can save himself or that he presumes his forgiveness from sins without conversion and glory without merit (*CCC* 2091–2092). This means that we should believe that God wills our salvation, consistent with the parable of the Prodigal Son, but that we cannot achieve it without His aid.

The first commandment also calls us to love God divinely — that is to say, with charity (*CCC* 2093). Finally, the first commandment beckons us to serve only the one true God, letting go of our worldly idols that stop us from serving Him fully, whether they be other gods or secular goods, such as money, pride, sports, or even laziness. Serving God alone is not easy for fallen man, whose first instinct is to serve himself. Still, God wills our salvation, regardless of what we've done or not done, just as is the case with the prodigal son. At the same time, God's grace can help us fulfill His commands.

"The second commandment *prescribes respect for the Lord's name*" (CCC 2142). It forbids the abuse of God's name, false oaths, perjury, and blasphemy against the Church, the saints, or holy objects (CCC 2146–2152). Such abuse is contrary to love, while respect is consistent with love.

The third commandment is to keep the Lord's Day holy, which includes attending Sunday Mass and holy days of obligation (CCC 2168). Failure to attend Mass on Sunday and holy days of obligation without a good reason (sickness) is a mortal sin because Jesus' Passion and death cost Him everything (CCC 2177–2178). It is also a sacrilege when we miss Mass and receive Holy Communion without properly getting back in the state of grace through the sacrament of Reconciliation (CCC 2120).

Jesus desires that we do good on the Sabbath, not that we do no work. He healed a crippled woman on the Sabbath and had to chastise the leader of the synagogue who complained about this "violation" (Luke 13:10–17). Similarly, the Pharisees complained that Jesus' disciples were picking grain on the Sabbath. Jesus responded, "If you knew what this meant, 'I desire mercy, not sacrifice,' you would not have condemned these innocent men. For the Son of Man is Lord of the sabbath" (Matt. 12:7–8). Jesus immediately proceeded into their synagogue, where He encountered a man with a withered hand. The Pharisees asked Jesus whether it was legal to cure on the Sabbath. Citing the story of a sheep who falls into a pit, Jesus concluded that "it is lawful to do good on the sabbath" and healed the man over the Pharisees' objections (Matt. 12:9–13). While the Sabbath was put in place to allow men to rest, it is lawful and right to do works of mercy on the Sabbath.

Sins against Order (the Fourth Commandment)

The fourth commandment extends from the parents to all those who legitimately exercise authority over others in any capacity. It is the duty of every person to show honor, affection, and gratitude to all those who have leadership roles over them (CCC 2199). It is the duty of those in leadership roles to serve those they lead, getting them the necessary resources to do their jobs well and helping them remove obstacles to their success (Matt. 20:26). If a leader asks the follower to do something that is immoral, the follower must call this to the leader's attention and refuse to do it. If the leader insists on immoral behavior, the followers are within their rights to replace the leader.

Order begins with the human family, which is the basic building block of society (CCC 2207). At the same time, the political community has an obligation to aid the family by ensuring the following:

- ✛ the freedom to establish a family, have children, and bring them up in keeping with the family's own moral and religious convictions;
- ✛ the protection of the stability of the marriage bond and the institution of the family;
- ✛ the freedom to profess one's faith, to hand it on, and raise one's children in it, with the necessary means and institutions;
- ✛ the right to private property, to free enterprise, to obtain work and housing, and the right to emigrate;
- ✛ in keeping with the country's institutions, the right to medical care, assistance for the aged, and family benefits;
- ✛ the protection of security and health, especially with respect to dangers like drugs, pornography, alcoholism, etc.;

✠ the freedom to form associations with other families
and so to have representation before civil authority.
(CCC 2211)

According to the *Catechism*, the fourth commandment *illuminates other relationships in society*. In our brothers and sisters we see the children of our parents; in our cousins, the descendants of our ancestors; in our fellow citizens, the children of our country; in the baptized, the children of our Mother, the Church; in every human person, a son or daughter of the One who wants to be called "our Father." In this way our relationships with our neighbors are recognized as personal in character. The neighbor is not a "unit "in the human collective; he is "someone" who by his known origins deserves particular attention and respect. (CCC 2212) This demonstrates the way we love others.

The fourth commandment also dictates the way family members relate to each other. Children's respect for their parents derives from gratitude over their gift of life and of work to raise and educate them (CCC 2215). As long as they live at home, children should obey their parents, except in the case where they are asked to do something morally wrong (against the Ten Commandments), which they should not do. This commandment also reminds grown children to act out of love for their aging parents, giving them material and moral support (CCC 2218). And this same love should extend among siblings.

The duties of parents include having the first responsibility for the education of the children in the practice of the virtues. "This requires an apprenticeship in self-denial, sound judgment, and self-mastery — the preconditions of all true freedom" (CCC 2223). I, like most first-time parents, was initially terrified of raising another human being. This is why God designed the family to entail two parents raising a child, so they can support each other. Child-rearing occurs best within a sacramental marriage. The sacrament of

Matrimony, of which God is the author, helps us to overcome self-absorption, egotism, and pursuit of our own pleasures by opening ourselves up to our spouse, to mutual aid, and to self-giving (*CCC* 1609). Holy Matrimony bestows God's aid and strength to a man and woman, enabling them to become good spouses and parents (*CCC* 1643). God's help is also available at a later time if a couple, who married secularly, chooses to have their marriage blessed by the Church. They must make the request of a priest or deacon, the ordinary ministers of this sacrament. This is yet another sign of God's great mercy.

Sins against Life (the Fifth Commandment)

Human life is sacred from conception to natural death (*CCC* 2258). This simple statement outlaws all use of embryos as genetic material, euthanasia, and any form of suicide or abortion. God alone is the Lord of life. To this commandment, "You shall not kill," Jesus adds the proscription against anger, hatred, and vengeance, and going further, He asks His disciples to love their enemies (*CCC* 2262).

The fifth commandment also protects against scandal, "an attitude or behavior which leads another to do evil" (*CCC* 2284). Scandal can be provoked by laws or institutions, by fashion or opinion. Those who establish laws or social structures leading to the decline of morals and the corruption of religious practice are guilty of scandal. They are responsible for the evil that is directly or indirectly encouraged (*CCC* 2285–2287).

The fifth commandment respects not only life but health. But it also "rejects a neo-pagan notion that tends to promote the *cult of the body*," such as "enhancements" that fit a societal ideal rather than God's design for that person (*CCC* 2289). At the same time, the commandment protects the virtue of temperance, which disposes us to avoid every kind of excess and leads to proper self-love (*CCC* 2290).

SINS AGAINST MARRIAGE (THE SIXTH COMMANDMENT)

Sex has unitive and procreative value that must not be separated, and it is properly ordered only in the covenant of marriage between a man and a woman. This simple statement is at the center of Catholic teaching and is the point of argumentation for the current "culture wars." Humanity has been undeniably separated into biological males and females for the purpose of procreation, and the creation of new human life is only possible through the merging of the gametes of the two sexes. The fact that this is biologically induced by God at the point of conception is shown by the inability of those who "change gender" medically to reproduce as the alternate gender. Changing one's gender is at best superficial, with hormone and surgical "reassignment" affecting the physical appearance but not the cellular structure of those involved. Changing the structure of every cell is tantamount to redesigning the whole person, which is well beyond modern science's capabilities. The integrity of the human person should never be modified, for each individual is designed perfectly for God's plan. When a person tries to alter him- or herself, then he or she becomes less able to fulfill his or her God-given potential.

Separating the unitive and procreative features of sex is what causes many artificial contraception and artificial fertility methods, including in vitro fertilization and surrogate motherhood, to be immoral (CCC 2366). Conjugal love is intended to be fruitful. Namely, spouses should be open to having and educating children as part of the unitive process. God blesses many husbands and wives with a child and gives them the grace to love and to raise that child as a way to bring the couple together. It is true that not everyone can reproduce naturally or even unnaturally, and this too is purposeful, because the Church teaches that having a child is a gift of marriage and not a right — categorizing parenthood as a right would brand a child as a commodity and dictate that a person could demand sex from another. In addition, the child would not be the *individual* he was designed to be (*CCC* 2378).

Marriage is the foundation for all human societies, and the responsibility of the parents is to teach children right from wrong and how to build relationships. Anything that dissuades married couples from having and raising children is immoral. Adultery is a grave sin; not only does it hurt the marital bond, but it also hurts society and the Church by being contrary to the welfare of the children (*CCC* 2381). Divorce is wrong for the same reasons, especially since God willed marriage to be permanent. The spouses can be morally separated by a civil divorce if that is the only way that certain civil rights can be protected. But no remarriage is possible without adultery (*CCC* 2382).

Sins against marriage include extramarital sex in all its forms without the lifetime commitment of marriage necessary for the raising of children (*CCC* 2390–2391). Polygamy negates the plan of God for equal personal dignity between men and women (*CCC* 2387). Incest involves intimate relations between relatives sufficiently close to lead to genetic defects and is a grave moral offense that also corrupts family relationships (*CCC* 2388).

Sins involving Property (the Seventh Commandment)

Based on love, the seventh commandment prohibits stealing but also covers unjustly taking or retaining the goods of another (*CCC* 2401). We are called to respect the goods and the needs of another and to return those we have taken unjustly (*CCC* 2409, 2412). This commandment also demands that contracts and even promises be kept (*CCC* 2410) and that people never cheat or hurt one another through wagers (*CCC* 2413). It also forbids any acts or enterprises that lead to the enslavement of human beings (*CCC* 2414).

The seventh commandment respects the goodness of creation. It is contrary to human dignity to cause an animal to suffer or die unnecessarily. Men have been entrusted with the stewardship of the earth and are responsible for the appropriate use of animal, vegetable, and mineral resources, considering the needs of our neighbors, including future generations (CCC 2415–2418).

Church social doctrine is also guided by this commandment. The Church makes a moral judgment about economic and social matters when the fundamental rights of the person or the salvation of souls requires it. For instance, the Church developed social teaching in response to the Industrial Revolution in the nineteenth century to rebalance the world more toward labor and away from a theory that made profit the exclusive norm and ultimate end of economic activity. In more recent times, the Church has rejected the totalitarian and atheistic ideologies associated with communism and socialism. Regulating the economy solely by central planning exaggerates man's perspective and foresight while perverting the basis of social bonds in love (CCC 2419–2425).

According to Catholic social and economic teaching, every person has the necessary skills and resources to fulfill his or her potential in God's plan. This requires that everyone has the right to economic initiative and the right to work. At the same time, the state is responsible for eliminating corruption and enabling all people to meet their potential. Businesses have the responsibility to hire without prejudice, to pay a living wage, and to consider the good of persons and not only the increase of profits. This is not to deny the importance of profits to a business, only to put it in perspective. It is also incumbent on workers to pay taxes and make social contributions required by legitimate authority (CCC 2426–2442) to serve the good of all.

The Church's love for the poor is part of her constant tradition. This love is inspired by the Beatitudes and the works of mercy. The spiritual works of mercy include instructing the ignorant, advising the sinner, counseling the doubtful, comforting the sorrowful, forgiving all injuries, bearing wrongs patiently, and praying for the living and the dead. The corporal works of mercy consist of feeding the hungry, giving drink to the thirsty, clothing the naked, sheltering the homeless, visiting the sick and the imprisoned, and burying the dead (CCC 2443–2447).

Sins involving the Truth (the Eighth Commandment)

The eighth commandment forbids misrepresenting the truth in our relationships with others. The truth comes from God, and people are compelled by their nature and by a moral obligation to seek the truth but especially religious truth. Without the truth, men cannot plan their activity with any degree of certainty, and therefore, telling falsehoods deprives the recipients of their just due. If the recipient is planning on using the truth to do evil, it is better to stay silent than to lie or to tell the truth. People are also compelled to keep secrets except in the case where an innocent person will be harmed (CCC 2465–2470).

The eighth commandment also calls for us to witness to the truth about Christ (CCC 2471–2475). Martyrdom is the supreme witness of faith whereby a person demonstrates the intensity of his love for Christ by offering his own life.

Offenses against truth include false witness and perjury, which contribute to the condemnation of the innocent and exoneration of the guilty (CCC 2476). "*Respect for the reputation* of persons forbids every attitude and word likely to cause them unjust injury" (CCC 2477). This includes rash judgment, detraction, and calumny. Flattery, adulation, and complaisance are forbidden because they encourage and confirm another in malicious acts and perverse conduct (CCC 2480). "*Boasting* or bragging is an offense against trust. So is *irony* aimed at disparaging someone by maliciously caricaturing some aspect of his behavior" (*CCC* 2481).

SINS AGAINST MODESTY (THE NINTH COMMANDMENT)

The ninth commandment forbids all bodily desires contrary to human reason, not just restraint from coveting another's spouse. This requires purity of heart and temperance. In short, it requires modesty. Modesty is decent and discreet in both language and attire, seeking neither to entice nor be enticed by that which would impair a person's spiritual dignity. Modesty treats a person as the image of God, not as an object of desire. This transcends culture, which may have different forms taken by modesty (*CCC* 2518–2524). Purity of heart brings freedom from widespread eroticism and avoids entertainment inclined to voyeurism and illusion (*CCC* 2525).

THE DISORDER OF COVETOUS DESIRES (THE TENTH COMMANDMENT)

The sensitive desires lead us to want pleasant things we do not have, like the desire to eat or to warm ourselves. Such desires are useful, but often they exceed the limits of reason and drive us to covet unjustly. The tenth commandment forbids greed and the desire to amass earthly goods without limit and without justice (*CCC* 2535–2537). Every person has the resources and skills to do God's will. When we covet others' possessions, we show ingratitude toward God and a lack of hope in His plan. Coveting can lead to idolatry when a person desires things more than he desires God and His Kingdom.

The Ten Commandments are all interrelated and synergistic with all Catholic doctrines, demonstrating their adherence to the truth. They are each discernible by reason. If a person struggles with the veracity of any of them, I suggest contemplating how violating them would offend God. At the same time, the Ten Commandments identify what is evil and, therefore, counter to love. The truth and goodness of the commandments will become clearer over time to the person who doubts but not to the person who denies. This is because the person in denial is not open to the truth, but the person who doubts is. It does no one any good to deny the truth because the truth tells us what is real and can be counted on to plan.

The natural law, which is the Ten Commandments known by reason, is the same for all men because it represents the truth of God's design. All humans who love their neighbors and God will recognize that the Ten Commandments codify that love, regardless of their faith. We are all looking for the truth because it tells us what can be trusted. Unlike opinion, truth is the same for everyone at any time and in any circumstance. This is because all truth comes from God and is real. It is not made up by men — it is discovered or, like the Ten Commandments, revealed by God. Considering that Moses walked down from Mt. Sinai after his theophany, carrying the Ten Commandments imprinted on stone tablets, written by God Himself, only adds to their credibility (Exod. 32:15–16).

Chapter 8

Sharing in the Divine Nature by Living the Beatitudes

AN ALTERNATE WAY TO understand love, the currency of Heaven, is to follow Jesus' example. From the Gospel accounts we can see how Jesus relates to different people in different situations. He also left us the gift of the Beatitudes, which the Church says "depict the countenance of Jesus Christ and portray his charity" (*CCC* 1717). Furthermore, "the Beatitudes respond to the natural desire for happiness. This desire is of divine origin: God has placed it in the human heart in order to draw man to the One who alone can fulfill it" (*CCC* 1718). The Beatitudes unveil the purpose of human existence: God calls us to share in His happiness, which makes us "'partakers of the divine nature' and of eternal life" (*CCC* 1719, 1721). Said another way, "God put us in the world to know, to love, and to serve Him, and so to come to paradise" (*CCC* 1721). The Beatitudes show us how to act divinely — that is, to act with charity.

When Jesus began the Sermon on the Mount with the Beatitudes, it undoubtedly sounded like a series of disjointed paradoxes to many in the crowd. Jesus uses an entirely different measurement system to define what makes a person happy. Then, as now, the "winners" of the world were the aggressors, the people who leverage every advantage to exploit their neighbors to get what they want. The thought that the meek would inherit the earth seemed unthinkable. Happy are the poor? What do they have to be happy about?

The Beatitudes, however, create a way of thinking and acting that will enhance all human relationships and lead to happiness — in this life, yes, but it will also create the kind of currency that you can take with you when you die: charity, your love of God, and through it, your love of your neighbors. They also put focus on some of the errors of modern thinking, exposing them as distortions of the truth. The Beatitudes show us divine love from eight perspectives, each of them working together and also with the rest of Catholic doctrine.

1. BLESSED ARE THE POOR IN SPIRIT, FOR THEIRS IS THE KINGDOM OF HEAVEN (MATT. 5:3)

The poor in spirit are those who put their trust in God rather than in material wealth. Jesus trusted in God as demonstrated by His ministry and His way of life. He was an itinerant preacher during His ministry, living off the donations of others. Twice Jesus sent out His disciples as missionaries with stern orders not to take anything but the clothes on their back for their journey, the first time with the twelve apostles (Luke 9:1–6), the second time with seventy-two others (Luke 10:1–12). Jesus wanted to instill the virtue of hope in His disciples: He would take care of them. Upon the disciples' return, Jesus said, "When I sent you forth without a money bag or a sack or sandals, were you in need of anything?" They replied, "No, nothing" (Luke 22:35).

This beatitude is a condemnation not so much of the wealthy as their priorities. Later in the Sermon on the Mount, Jesus explained that "no one can serve two masters. He will either hate one and love the other, or be devoted to one and despise the other. You cannot serve God and mammon" (Matt 6:24).[84] Jesus further declares that we should first seek the Kingdom of Heaven and should trust in God to provide for all our material needs (Matt. 6:25–33). This beatitude

---

[84] Note, *mammon* is an Aramaic word translated as "wealth" or "property" according to the NABRE notes explaining Matthew 6:24.

is consistent with the first commandment and the greatest commandment. This beatitude is also the antithesis of Original Sin, which puts man's desire first.

To be poor in spirit does not deny that we must live in this world. In fact, God made us its stewards (Gen. 1:26). God also gave each of us certain skills that can be used for the betterment of the world — using these gifts for others is at the heart of this beatitude. If we think about our occupations and activities as conduits by which we manifest God's love, then we can move from selfishness to selflessness. As long as love dictates the way we relate to others, there is no need for rules because every member is committed to each other and the good of the group. Sin, mostly self-centeredness, often forces organizations to develop rules of conduct. Policing functions, judgment, and punishment soon follow to enforce the rules as more love is lost and people only react to avoid punishment.

It is no surprise that the Kingdom of God belongs to the poor in spirit because they value the love of God, Heaven's currency, above all else. The person who is poor in spirit will use his resources to help the poor, showing solidarity with them. Jesus conveys this point when interacting with Zacchaeus, a rich tax collector in Jericho. Elated upon being told by Jesus that He was going to stay with him, Zacchaeus promised to give half of his money to the poor and to give back four times whatever he defrauded. Jesus responded by declaring, "Today salvation has come to this house" (Luke 19:1–10). This shows us God's forgiveness and His priority system. Indeed, Zacchaeus was saved because he acted out of love toward the poor, using his great wealth charitably, not because he had wealth to begin with.

People who prize the love of God above everything will be happy in this life and in the next. Those who trust in material wealth will never be satisfied here and will likely find themselves outside God's Kingdom in the next. A person who is poor in spirit makes decisions out of love, not for material gain. He will sympathize with all people, regardless of social or economic status, and seek to help them because that is what God's love motivates us to do.

God has inspired many wealthy individuals to be poor in spirit, even among the saints. These men and women were chosen for roles in God's plans just like the people they served. Both situations are part of God's plans. Sometimes wealthy people are chosen to renounce their riches and embrace God in discomfort. Such was the situation for Francis Bernardone, the son of a wealthy cloth merchant in Assisi. St. Francis of Assisi deliberately led a life of poverty to teach the Church to be poor in spirit when she was focused too much on the material world.[85]

Philadelphia native St. Katharine Drexel was the heiress of a massive fortune in the late nineteenth century. She did not renounce her fortune but used it to fund a ministry for the advancement of underprivileged minorities (particularly African Americans and Native Americans).[86]

The Catholic Church has canonized kings and queens for being poor in spirit and for caring for the sick and poor in their realms. Two of the most prominent of these were inspired by St Francis of Assisi: St. Elizabeth, queen of Hungary, and St. Louis IX, king of France, both of whom personally served hundreds of the poor on a regular basis.[87] In a pious letter to his eldest son and heir on his twenty-first birthday, St. Louis IX wrote "The first thing I advise is that you fix your whole heart upon God, and love Him with all your strength, for without this no one can be saved or be of any worth."[88]

[85] Paschal Robinson, "St. Francis of Assisi," *The Catholic Encyclopedia*, vol. 6 (New York: Robert Appleton Company, 1909), http://www.newadvent.org/cathen/06221a.htm.

[86] "St. Katharine Drexel," Catholic Online, https://www.catholic.org/saints/saint.php?saint_id=193.

[87] "St. Louis IX," Catholic Online, https://www.catholic.org/saints/saint.php?saint_id=1011.

[88] Louis IX, "Advice of St. Louis to His Son," in *Medieval Civilization*, trans. and ed. Dana Munro and George Clarke Sellery (New York: The Century

For the vast majority of society, who are neither in poverty nor independently wealthy, there are ways to be poor in spirit. Included in this is cultivating the habit of not treating people with wealth better than we treat those in poverty. St. James warned against the sin of partiality, where a person is shown favoritism because of his wealth and the poor person is discriminated against (James 2:1–13). Indeed, when we show deference to the wealthy, it is a sign that we want their favor and hope to depend on them rather than on God. This is even more foolhardy than depending on our own wealth since we will never be the top priority of wealthy benefactors. Further, when we despise someone who can do us no favors, then we are failing to love them.

People of all economic levels can convert their material assets to heavenly ones through charity. Note that this is true charity only if it is done to align with God's plan and in solidarity with the recipient. Motivation matters. Jesus says explicitly that if you do righteous acts in order for people to see them, you will receive no spiritual credit because you already have received the reward you sought (Matt. 6:1). Bad intentions corrupt good actions, just as good intentions don't justify evil acts (CCC 1750–1755). If the action and its intention are both good, then the act is ordered to God and will result in joy.

Note, Jesus also describes a poor widow giving two small coins as having more value than the huge sums of money being given by the wealthy out of their surplus. He explains that the woman had sacrificed all she had to live on while the others gave what they did not need (Luke 21:1–4). Her self-giving love is not only strong but also redemptive because she suffers for another.

Company, 1910), 366–375.

2. Blessed are they who mourn, for they will be comforted (Matt. 5:4)

People typically mourn when they lose someone or something of value, especially a loved one. When Jesus experienced the loss of his dear friend Lazarus, He wept (John 11:35). Even the Jews of the day recognized mourning as a sign of love, for they comment on Jesus' tears: "See how he loved him" (John 11:36). But Jesus is also the consoler, so He raised Lazarus from the dead (John 11:44).

Jesus also mourns over the state of Jerusalem, whose inhabitants killed the prophets and stoned those sent to them. He laments that He wanted to gather their children together but they were unwilling, so their homes will be abandoned, and they will not see Him again until they say, "Blessed is he who comes in the name of the Lord" (Matt. 23:37–39). If we care enough to mourn the loss of love in this world or the loss of a loved one, and we love and trust God, then Jesus can console us in the same way; He can raise us and our loved ones on the Last Day. This promise alone is consoling, but it requires that we and our loved ones reach Heaven. With this in mind, we must help our loved ones to build up heavenly currency.

An interesting dynamic involves the mourning of the unjust who end up in Hell. These poor souls have separated themselves from God and thus can no longer participate in charity. As we have learned from St. Thomas Aquinas, in charity, we love those most who are either near to us or near to God. Since the damned are far from God, they could be mourned by only very close family and associates and only for a relatively short time. Eventually, mourning will cease to exist. The lack of charity adds to the bleakness of Hell.

3. Blessed are the meek, for they will inherit the land (Matt. 5:5)

The third beatitude is based on our own self-awareness. The meek put others' needs before their own and know their place in society and in God's plan. They strive to do God's will and not force their will on others. Jesus set the standard: "Take my yoke upon you and learn from me, for I am meek and humble of heart; and you will find rest for yourselves. For my yoke is easy, and my burden light" (Matt. 11:29–30). In other words, meekness and humility enable our tasks to seem light because God will give us the necessary resources and training to succeed. When we usurp a role meant for someone else, we will struggle because God never intended that position for us. The meek therefore show their love for God through their fidelity to His plan.

They might also show fidelity to His plan by putting others' needs above their own. For instance, if you were a nurse practicing this beatitude, you would be willing to stay a little longer or miss a break if your patient needed your support, regardless of payment. If you were a clerk in a store and someone needed something at closing time, you would help them get what they needed out of love for them and God, even if it delayed your plans. If you were a teacher, you would put your students' needs before your own. Clearly, the meek demonstrate redemptive love by loving God and others more than themselves.

The arrogant, however, put their own desires above the needs of others. They cause suffering by exploiting others for their own gain. The arrogant will have no place in the Kingdom of God because they are storing up useless material treasure instead of building charity, which is Heaven's currency.

4. Blessed are they who hunger and thirst for righteousness, for they will be satisfied (Matt. 5:6)

Righteousness means conduct in conformity with God's will in Matthew's Gospel.[89] This means that a person living this beatitude desires to both know and implement God's plan. God has provided three ways to know what constitutes righteousness. First, He embedded in our consciences the ability to judge right from wrong. St. Paul calls this the interior law (Rom. 2:12–16). Second, the Church offers great wisdom compiled from the revelations to prophets, apostles, saints, and most specifically through Jesus' words and actions in the Gospels. Finally, suffering is one of our greatest teachers. Evil (unrighteous) actions cause suffering while righteous actions alleviate or avoid suffering.

The person seeking righteousness must recognize the truth from the distortions prevalent in a society that has lost its moral compass. The problem with made-up "truths" is that you cannot plan or act on them because they contradict real truths, causing confusion, injustices, and suffering.

One prevalent distortion is that all men were created equal and that, to be fair, all people must be treated the same. Neither of these things are true, even if many people believe them and even though they are enshrined in the United States' Declaration of Independence.[90] What is undeniably true is every one of God's creations is unique, fashioned lovingly to be perfect for the role that God has intended. This is true regarding every human being, from society's most celebrated leaders and heroes to the least skilled, most dependent individuals, and is easily observed by anyone who is

---

[89] See the NABRE Scripture note for Matthew 5:10.
[90] "Declaration of Independence: A Transcription," America's Founding Documents, National Archives, accessed 12/10/2022, https://www.archives.gov/founding-docs/declaration-transcript.

fair-minded. While everyone has equal dignity as a child of God with his own assigned role in God's plan, individuals are not equal in any other way. This is the distortion.

The most successful leaders realize that everyone possesses unique skills, resources, and interests. These make us not equal. The greatest leaders put their subordinates in the best roles, leading to happy customers and employees. Everyone prospers because this is how God designed it to be. This puts good personnel managers at a premium because they can find ways to help people find their niches. This makes everyone happy — everyone, that is, except those fueled by pride and envy, who desire the perks and pay of someone else's position without recognizing the responsibilities of the position or their lack of qualifications for it. These people are focused on material gain and have not bothered to discern what God wants for them, which is what will really make them happy and enable them to build the kind of intense love for God and others that is Heaven's currency.

Imagine another alternative where the manager believes that all people are created equal, and they should all be treated the same. Instead of working to discern his employees' strengths and weaknesses, he assigns everyone a job each morning at random. Productivity would be a fraction of what it could be, and people would be very unhappy. Perhaps these individuals would be overwhelmed by a job they were unqualified for and underequipped to carry out. Perhaps they would be bored because they were overqualified for the job assigned to them. Even the people who were randomly selected for their ideal jobs would be unhappy because the enterprise as a whole would fail.

Recognizing the truth of God's plan is critical to even secular success. Truth is truth. This can be shown from a worker's standpoint too. Workers seek appealing jobs because they pay well. But if they do not have the required skills or training, a competent manager will never hire them. If they are hired, they will inevitably struggle and fail to be as productive as employees made for that job. Ironically, the loving thing for the manager to do is to fire the employee who is in the wrong job and get them aid in finding the job that was meant for them. Unfortunately, few managers today would follow up like this for employees they fire, and, in some cases, they might be chastised by their own management for doing so.

In God's plan, everyone has needs, requiring cooperation between individuals to do anything of value. This cooperation, if done without expectation of payment, is love. As children of God, we deserve to love and be loved according to our particular needs. Again, this beatitude is anchored in charity, our love and friendship with God. Treating everyone equally is insufficient to meet the needs of all, because some have inherently greater needs than others and all have some uniquely individual needs. To be righteous is to help others meet their needs, to the best of our abilities, often requiring some self-sacrifice. When people sacrifice for others, they are rewarded with joy.

The problem with modern society, both collectively and individually, is that it seeks to create its own reality, one that meets the individual desires of its members. This stems from Original Sin, whereby we choose our will over God's will. Adam and Eve faced the same scenario in the Garden of Eden. Those who hunger and thirst for righteousness will reject the idea that truth is dependent on the opinions of individuals and that man decides what is right and wrong. Despite having clear direction from God and the Church, many believe Satan's false gospel of lies.

This deception occurs because people are constantly judging themselves against others rather than against their own potential as God grades us. If we perceive that we have been given a less visible or less important role than someone else, we consider it unfair and rebel against God. This is mostly pride, but it reflects some insecurity about how we are viewed by others. It is also misdirected and ungrateful because God gives us the skills to carry out our roles and we are made perfectly for them, whereas someone else was made perfectly for the roles we ungratefully desire. God judges us according to how well we use our gifts and abilities to create love according to His plan. More is expected of those who have more (Luke 12:48). This reemphasizes that we are to be meek, satisfied with the role God made us for but doing it to the best of our ability.

Righteousness demands that people are not arbitrarily discriminated against for any reason whatsoever. At the same time, it is not just for an unqualified person to claim an equal right to any role. That would be a disordered choice, the very definition of sin.[91] The righteous love God, so they want to adhere to His plan, which they trust is best for them (this is the theological virtue of hope). People who want fairness will ultimately be satisfied with carrying out God's plan for them, whether the role be large or small, because that is what they were meant to do, and they will find it both satisfying and easy to do.

The way a person following the Beatitudes would price his services would be governed by the fourth beatitude. It would be based on meeting both the customer's and the provider's needs, trusting in God and our neighbors that no one is asking for anything beyond their needs.

5. Blessed are the merciful, for they will be shown mercy (Matt. 5:7)

Mercy involves both kindness and forgiveness; it gives a person more consideration than they think they deserve. Jesus' ministry was full of mercy. He healed the sick and drove out demons (Matt. 9:35–38), but He also ate with tax collectors and sinners (Luke 5:27–32), the outcasts of society. He forgave the woman caught in adultery (John 7:53–8:11) and the men who crucified Him (Luke 23:34).

---

[91] *ST* I-II, q. 75, art. 1.

Jesus' key qualification for His final judgment involves whether we show mercy to the least of our brothers by feeding the hungry, giving drink to the thirsty, clothing the naked, welcoming the stranger, caring for the ill, and visiting those in prison (Matt. 25:31–46). All of these things require that we give up our time and resources for the good of another. These are all forms of charity, which is ultimately motivated by the love of God. Therefore, we can build our love by practicing mercy as Jesus did, giving others the benefit of the doubt, forgiving all injuries, and carrying out the corporal and spiritual works of mercy. In the parable of the Last Judgment, Jesus is explicit in saying that those entering the Kingdom will carry out merciful acts for the least of our brothers (Matt. 25:31–46).

6. Blessed are the clean of heart, for they will see God (Matt. 5:8)

The clean of heart have not allowed themselves to be stained by sin. They are pure of mind and body. They see God in others, meaning they see what is good, not what is sinful. They dress and speak modestly, neither tempting nor being tempted by unchaste things or people. As Jesus says later in the Sermon on the Mount, it is not enough that one avoids committing adultery; one must refrain from even looking at another lustfully (Matt. 5:27–28). The clean of heart are innocent, looking only to do God's will. St. Paul emphasizes this to the Colossians, calling on them "to put to death, then, the parts of you that are earthly: immorality, impurity, passion, evil desire, and the greed that is idolatry" (Col. 3:5). He continues:

> Put on then, as God's chosen ones, holy and beloved, heartfelt compassion, kindness, humility, gentleness, and patience, bearing with one another and forgiving one another, if one has a grievance against another; as the Lord has forgiven you, so must you also do. And over all these put on love, that is, the bond of perfection. And let the

peace of Christ control your hearts, the peace into which you were also called in one body. And be thankful. Let the word of Christ dwell in you richly, as in all wisdom you teach and admonish one another, singing psalms, hymns, and spiritual songs with gratitude in your hearts to God. (Col. 3:12–16)

The clean of heart, those who have followed Jesus by loving Him and avoiding mortal sin, will have built up the intensity of love (Heaven's currency) to enter into God's Kingdom, where they will experience the ultimate joy of seeing God as He truly is.

7. Blessed are the peacemakers, for they will be called children of God (Matt. 5:9)

Being a peacemaker is not about compromising the truth to placate others; rather, it centers on handling conflict. Jesus Himself is the cause for great division in the world. He even says that He did not come to bring peace but the sword, setting a man against his father and a daughter against her mother (Matt. 10:34–35). Nor did Jesus hesitate to denounce those who opposed the will of God, calling the scribes and Pharisees blind guides, hypocrites, and worse, saddling them with seven woes or grievances about their conduct (Matt. 23).

In the Sermon on the Mount, Jesus offers a radical view of a peacemaker: one who acts in love toward his adversaries (Matt. 5:43–47). Jesus tells us that not only killing our adversaries is wrong but to be angry with them leaves us liable to judgment (Matt. 5:21–22). Furthermore, He advises us to offer no resistance to one who is evil but to instead turn the other cheek rather than retaliating (Matt. 5:38–42).

So how do we reconcile all of this? One of the spiritual works of mercy is to correct the sinner (CCC 2447). This is an act of love because it gives them the opportunity to repent and be saved. This is what Jesus was doing with the scribes and Pharisees. This is critically important because many people today believe it is better to affirm one in his errors than to correct him with the truth because it will cause less conflict. This is lying, the opposite of showing love, and not only will it result in more poor decisions, but it will also not lead to repentance and spiritual growth.

But an even more profound way to be a peacemaker is for an aggrieved party to love their oppressors enough to socialize their sufferings, so their oppressors understand the harm they are doing and their consciences force them to repent. This method of peacemaking has been practiced in the last century by Mahatma Gandhi in overturning British colonialism in both South Africa and India and by Dr. Martin Luther King Jr. in easing racial segregation in the United States. Gandhi commented that this method exchanged hatred for pity.[92] Dr. King explained:

> We will match your capacity to inflict suffering with our capacity to endure suffering. We will meet your physical force with soul force....We will soon wear you down by our capacity to suffer and in winning our freedom we will so appeal to your heart and conscience that we will win you in the process.[93]

This radical view of peacemaking is not only useful for huge societal problems, but it can also be employed in any situation where one party is exploiting another. Specifically, if the oppressed party can show the oppressor what they have become in a loving way, the oppressor's conscience will be engaged, and in most cases they will repent. No one wants to see themselves as a monster. As seen throughout this book, God uses suffering to bring about salvation. Those practicing

---

[92]   Mahatma Gandhi, *The Essential Gandhi: An Anthology of His Writings on His Life, Work, and Ideas,* ed. Louis Fischer (New York: Vintage, 2002), 134.

[93]   Gary Commins, "Is Suffering Redemptive? Historical and Theological Reflections on Martin Luther King Jr.," *Sewanee Theological Review* 51, no. 1 (Christmas 2007): 62.

this method of peacemaking are called children of God because they are sharing in the divine nature, suffering for the good of others, which is redemptive (1 Pet. 4:13).

8: Blessed are they who are persecuted for the sake of righteousness, for theirs is the kingdom of heaven (Matt. 5:10)

The willingness to suffer for what is right is part of this beatitude and the previous one. Embracing the cross is a sign of the individual's commitment to God and the strength of his love. Jesus' Passion and death revealed a level of intense love that is incomprehensible to man. He asks us to take up our own crosses and follow Him. He warns that "whoever wishes to save his life will lose it, but whoever loses his life for my sake will find it" (Matt. 16:25). This passage is more about giving up your own will and accepting God's will than it is a call to martyrdom. For those people willing to suffer and even die for God (the proof of the highest love possible), God promises Paradise. At the same time, if the person attempts to save his own life rather than help those in need, then he will be condemned, just as Jesus warns in the parable of the Last Judgment (Matt. 25:31–46).

As described above, the Beatitudes show us how to love as Jesus loved. The Beatitudes, however, will only be understood if we get beyond the assumptions made by people who do not know God and if we see that our true happiness waits for us in Heaven. For believers, the Beatitudes make perfect sense because they are consistent with all other Church doctrine. This is because they all speak the truth.

Note that all these doctrines build on each other from a few simple truths:

1. God is all-good and all-powerful.

2. God made man in His image to know, love, and serve Him by carrying out our roles in His plan.

3. God is perfect and has no needs, so humans show their love
   of God by loving and serving each other.

As Thomas Aquinas clarifies in his analysis in the *Summa*, love is a type of friendship that must be shared.[94] If it is not shared, then we all know that this is a tragedy, causing great pain for the one who loves alone. To love is to want to share your life with your beloved and to do whatever you can to make them happy because doing so leads to joy.

It is the same with us and God. As Jesus taught with the parable of the Prodigal Son, God loves us and wants us to return to Him for our happiness; just being in His presence provides for every human need and desire and, therefore, our complete and total happiness. He made us so we can share in His nature and in His life, so that we can know and love Him in a way that reflects, but not as fully, the way He knows and loves us.

Love does not have the same properties if it is not freely given, so we were all granted free will and reason to figure out what we want. God does not force us to love anyone, not even Himself, for this reason. God did, however, show us how He wanted us to love through Jesus' words and examples.

First, like any lover, He demands that He be the center of our lives. This is explained in the first commandment and the first beatitude, and in fact all love begins with God, who is its source. As St. John describes it, "God is love" (1 John 4:8). He wants us to care so much for His plan and each other that we mourn when either is hurt or lost. He wants us to put others' needs before our own and to work for what is right, even if we suffer as a result. To be effective peacemakers, we need to be prepared for self-sacrifice because true love always involves self-giving. To enter God's Kingdom, we need to think and act without sin, staying in the state of grace until death. If we sin and need God's mercy, we must be merciful to others.

[94] *ST* I-II, q. 28, art. 1.

In the end, what Jesus shows us with the Beatitudes is a different way of thinking about our lives and how we live them. Instead of focusing on our needs, we focus on the needs of others, not for self-gain but for their gain and for the good of God's plan, even if we do not understand its meaning. It is enough for us that God wishes it because we trust in His goodness and His love for us. We see that everything God does is for the salvation of His children, and we seek to close the loop and return that love with our every action.

We also see that the Beatitudes show us eight different ways to express our love but that all of these ways express the same reality: giving of ourselves to improve the lives we share with others for the glory of God. This is consistent with the Ten Commandments. We realize that this way to love is a gift to us from God and that the more we practice it, the more joyous we feel and the more intense the motivation becomes to keep doing it. This is God infusing our souls with the theological virtues of faith, hope, and charity. But as St. Paul wrote to the Corinthians, it is charity that animates the other virtues, just as it is charity that is the true currency of Heaven (1 Cor. 13:1–13).

CHAPTER 9

THE WORKS OF MERCY

JESUS EMPHASIZED THE IMPORTANCE of the fifth beatitude when He told the parable of the Last Judgment (also called the Judgment of the Nations — Matt. 25:31–46). He describes the Last Judgment, explaining that when He comes in glory, He will separate the nations before Him as a shepherd separates the sheep from the goats, with the sheep on his right and the goats on his left. The sheep served Jesus (God) every time they aided the least among them (understood as the neediest). They are told they will enter Heaven because they gave food to Jesus when He was hungry and drink when He was thirsty, because they welcomed Him when He was a stranger and clothed Him when He was naked, because they cared for Him when He was ill and visited Him when He was in prison. The righteous wonder when they saw Jesus in such a state, but He tells them, "Whatever you did for one of these least brothers of mine, you did for me" (Matt. 25:40). This single statement shows that God commiserates with those who are needy and suffering and that to love them is to love Him. It is also interesting to see that it is their suffering that distinguishes who is in need and calls to those who are capable of love, like the Good Samaritan, to take action (Luke 10:29–37).

Jesus then turns to the unrighteous, whom He has moved to His left, and repeats the conversation, except that these He condemns to Hell because of their failure to aid those in need. Those who have no empathy for individuals in need will go off to eternal punishment, while those who did have empathy (the righteous) will go to the Kingdom prepared for them since the beginning of time (Matt. 25:31–46).

This call to be merciful to others emphasizes the fifth beatitude by focusing our attention on the least of our brothers, and it defines our treatment of them as the criteria to enter Heaven. Conversely, failure to help those in need is an affront to God and, if not reconciled, will exclude a person from His Kingdom. Jesus makes that very clear in this parable.

The ramifications of the Last Judgment are worth exploring. Many of the affluent have isolated themselves from the needy and thus will have to seek them out to be saved. Visiting a prison, a nursing home, or a hospital will take most of us outside our comfort zone and will cause us to sacrifice our time and perhaps some of our money. It will seem awkward until we have actually done it. Some envision having nothing to talk about, but that is not true. People in institutions are like anyone else — they like to talk about themselves, and they are generally grateful that anyone is interested enough to listen. It is good for their self-esteem; they will be appreciative, and both of you will feel joyful afterwards. The opposite will be true if the visitor talks only about himself, which in most cases comes off as self-serving and of little interest to the patient.

This sharing of yourself can also be done within the institution. My mother, Dolly Chaloux, resided at an assisted-living facility in the final years of her life, which coincided with the COVID-19 pandemic. The lockdown of the facilities caused great hardship for the patients and their families, who were not allowed to visit except for weekly Zoom calls. My mother was suffering from dementia and acute loneliness. One of her fellow residents, Kathy (I never met her, and I don't have her last name), saw this and kindly read to my mother for an hour almost every day. Although my mother was no longer able to communicate verbally and we were not there to witness it, the staff members told us that my mother's face would light up when Kathy was there. I can imagine that my mother was overjoyed by this personal contact, as would be anyone else in her position.

Most people, me included, do not take the time to show others such simple acts of kindness. We can all offer companionship (paying attention to someone else), regardless of our circumstances and state of life. Now, it may be hard to initiate such contact, particularly if you have never done it. It helps if you have a way to introduce yourself. Perhaps someone who is visiting a relative or who is part of a church group that already visits can help you overcome any awkwardness. Helping someone else may cost us some hardship, but it is never an excuse for not doing it. A simple act of kindness can change a life and save a soul, maybe our own. Let me be honest: This is one of those occasions when the realization comes to me that I don't love nearly as fully as I should. It makes me feel like a hypocrite, but I know I need to write this for the benefit of others who also haven't done enough for those who are lonely.

By emphasizing the importance of caring for those who suffer, Jesus teaches us to love, reminding us that what we do for the needy, we do for Him. We owe God everything because all that we have and are belongs to Him alone. Obtaining Paradise requires us to love God and all that is good, true, and beautiful in the universe. The parable of the Last Judgment provides a stark reminder on how to live according to the divine nature, which in turn validates the fifth beatitude. If we want to receive God's mercy at the hour of our death, we must show mercy to others while we are alive.

CHAPTER 10

LOVING THOSE WHO
DISAGREE WITH US

ONE OF THE GREATEST trials of love is dealing with people who disagree with us, because it tests not only our faith but also our understanding of how the Ten Commandments, the Beatitudes, and the works of mercy apply toward these situations. One area that many find particularly vexing is children, spouses, and parents who disagree with us on fundamental tenets of the Faith. For instance, children who refuse to attend Mass or have a sacramental marriage can cause great suffering. Often good parents feel a great deal of guilt over this, perhaps even blaming themselves. This can be the case if they have failed to educate their children in the Faith, as required by the fourth commandment, but parental lapses are often not the issue.

A major problem is that parents don't treat their adult children with the respect due other adults, which is also covered by the fourth commandment. Once a child has reached adulthood (around eighteen years old for reasoning ability and life experience), the now-adult child will be responsible for his own decisions and should be free to make them without undue pressure from his parents to conform to the parents' beliefs. Although many parents feel intense guilt when their children no longer practice the Faith, this feeling is misplaced if they have taught and lived the Faith. Indeed, if our children don't have the opportunity to love God of their own volition, they cannot be saved. It is necessary that they experience God's love firsthand and make the choice to act in charity toward Him and their neighbors, because nothing can force another person to love since love must be self-giving to be redemptive. Instead of worrying for their souls, we should pray and trust that God will continue to reach out to them, even at the moment of death, and that He wants us to be united in Paradise.

Disagreements on any issues with other adults, whether they be close family members or not, should be approached with mutual respect and understanding. This is governed by the seventh beatitude, which calls on us to be peacemakers (Matt. 5:9). Both sides should be open to understanding why the other has taken the position they have and what the stakes are for maintaining that position. In some cases, one person may conclude that the other person's reasoning is better than their own and they will be converted.

This is the optimum result, but it should be neither the expectation nor the source of sorrow if it is not achieved. In many cases, each of us forms positions based on our unique prior life experiences, and our perspectives are only understandable from that particular vantage point. At the same time, some points are a matter of taste and experience and have no definitive right or wrong answer, which may be inconvenient at times. No one should be forced to do something they do not like, and loving people will bear inconvenience to accommodate each other.

It is also true that discussing the matter may highlight the fact that the choice will affect one party more than the other. Although decisions affecting both parties should be made jointly, the resolution should reflect the common good, balancing the needs and desires of each while not exploiting either. In cases where the common good remains unclear, the loving action involves conceding to the other party, especially if there is no way to settle the impasse. Ultimately, we are called to bear wrongs patiently, a spiritual work of mercy.

The worst, least productive way to resolve a disagreement is to assume you are right and ignore the dissenting view. Depending on the dynamics involved, there are very different ramifications. If yours is the minority opinion, you will find yourself isolated from the others, without the possibility of convincing them. If yours is the majority opinion, whether it is ultimately right or wrong, you are inflicting suffering on the dissenters and probably hardening their anger against you, which is the antithesis of love.

Even more damaging is the modern tactic of punishing dissenting views with economic boycotts. This must be isolated from refusing to cooperate with evil, which is not only licit but a required moral action. The difference is intent. If a person boycotts a business to cause suffering for the owners and employers, that is evil, a violation of the third beatitude, which calls for us to be meek and not push our beliefs on anyone. This is much different than refusing to do business with people whose actions will cause suffering and instead favoring a company that avoids such evil. This is a good and is to be applauded. However, this can disguise bigotry, and it is never okay to cause social isolation or economic ruin out of bigotry, punishing another individual not for any evil that he has done but because he or she is different from us in some way. This fails to recognize that everyone is an individual, made perfectly and uniquely by God for his specific role in God's plan.

Pope St. John Paul II explained in his encyclical *Veritatis Splendor* that in evaluating actions, the object of the action (what the person is doing) must be good for an action to be good. The intention of the action (why it is being done) must also be good for an action to be good. However, a bad action can never be justified by a good intention. The circumstances, including the result of the action, cannot change the action from good to bad or from bad to good but can mitigate or increase responsibility for an action. In addition, actions often have undesired side effects that are not part of the moral calculus (the principle of double effect).

We can use this evaluation process (CCC 1750–1761), which dates back to St. Thomas Aquinas in the thirteenth century, to evaluate actions we can take when people disagree with us. Consider the action of not doing business with a person we disagree with. This is a morally neutral act because there is nothing inherently wrong with doing business with whomever you like. Motivation does matter, however. If you are motivated by a good intention — to avoid cooperating with evil, for instance — the action of boycotting a business is justified. On the other hand, if your motivation is evil — for example, to force a person to take an action they feel is unjust or if the action harms someone — then the action is unjust.

It should be noted that action theory is meant to evaluate one's own actions rather than another person's actions. This is because of the difficulty in evaluating another person's intentions and motivations. When people disagree with us, we can be too quick to assume bad intentions are at the root of their actions. Instead, we need to follow the example of Christ.

First of all, we should give others the benefit of the doubt on their intentions and trust in God to apply mercy and justice as appropriate. "Stop judging, that you may not be judged" (Matt. 7:1). At the same time, we should follow our conscience and not cooperate with evil, assuming that others are doing the same. We should never force others to violate their conscience, even when we think they are wrong (CCC 1782). We should, however, judge our own actions, and if we feel that we have taken unjust actions, we should rectify them as appropriate (CCC 1781). In this way we demonstrate proper love for others, even those we vehemently disagree with, always seeing them in a positive light and doing what is best for their souls.

Once we take an action, we must move on. Following the corporal works of mercy, we must forgive all injuries and bear wrongs patiently (CCC 2447). If the action caused us to suffer, we must love our neighbor enough to let him see the harm he has done, trusting that his conscience will engage and lead him to repentance (Matt. 5:43–48). Even in this case, we should be merciful, not seeking revenge (Matt 5:38–42). It should be enough for us if the oppression stops. It is evil to wish harm on anyone, even an oppressor (CCC 2262).

Charity, the love of others for God's sake, is the currency of Heaven, and increasing the depth and breadth of our love bonds us more tightly to God, leading to joy.

CHAPTER 11

HEAVEN'S CURRENCY

Do not store up for yourselves treasures on earth, where moths and decay destroy, and thieves break in and steal. But store up treasures in heaven, where neither moth nor decay destroys, nor thieves break in and steal. For where your treasure is, there also will your heart be.

— Matthew 6:19–21

IN THIS SHORT PASSAGE (on the previous page) from the Sermon on the Mount, Jesus confirms that there has to be a currency that carries over to Heaven because He tells us not to store up treasures on earth, which are temporary, but to store up treasure in Heaven. What, then, is this currency by which we store up treasure in Heaven? What would be its attributes?

Any currency that is good in Heaven must be spiritual, not material, since there is nothing physical in Heaven. Nor would it be used to buy goods or services, because God will provide for our every need through the Beatific Vision (*CCC* 1028). This means that what treasures we store up in Heaven are used to get us in. Does that mean we can buy our way into Heaven? Not at all. Nor can we work our way into Heaven without the grace of God, as the Pelagians claimed.[95] Indeed, true love comes from and is ordered to God. It is by God's grace, infused into our souls so that we can access it, but for us to love, we must freely decide and carry out God's will. When we do so, God strengthens the love within us by infusing more into our souls.

In economics, currency describes that which is legally used to transfer value between entities. There are two basic types of currency.

[95]   Joseph Pohle, "Pelagius and Pelagianism," *The Catholic Encyclopedia*, vol. 11 (New York: Robert Appleton Company, 1911), http://www.newadvent.org/cathen/11604a.htm.

One type has value of its own, while the second type has no intrinsic value, just the government's backing. In the former type, the currency will lose its intrinsic value if supply exceeds demand for it. "Soft" currency will lose its value if faith in the government's ability to guarantee its value versus commodities, services, or other currencies is lost.

Love is the only thing that has intrinsic value in both Heaven and earth, and supply never exceeds demand anywhere, so its value will stay high. Nothing else on earth transcends death, so the value to a person of any earthly accumulations becomes zero at the time of death. Therefore, to get any benefit for any earthly accumulation, we must convert those earthly assets (wealth, power, fame) into love while we live and they still have value to us. We must give of ourselves, which is not something that can be done with a will after we are dead.

We need to learn to love everyone we encounter. St. Teresa of Calcutta explained how this could be done: "Let no one ever come to you without leaving better and happier. Be the living expression of God's kindness: kindness in your face, kindness in your eyes, kindness in your smile."[96]

As said a few chapters back, the way to make ourselves more lovable as well as to love more fully is to share in the divine nature. Living according to the Beatitudes, which are further clarified by the Ten Commandments and the works of mercy, allows us to accomplish this and to be the living expression of God's kindness. As previously discussed, we can even gain the love of our oppressors by lovingly showing them how their actions are causing us to suffer and giving them the opportunity to repent.

If we choose to give of ourselves in every relationship, being willing to sacrifice for the good of the other, we will be practicing charity,

---

[96] Mother Teresa, *Mystics, Visionaries, and Prophets: A Historical Anthology of Women's Spiritual Writing*, ed. by Shawn Madigan. (MN: Augsburg Fortress, 1998), 423.

accumulating Heaven's currency for ourselves by depleting our earthly treasure, which will be totally worthless to us after we die. We will then experience the joy of spiritual growth, which is priceless.

This extends from giving money to the homeless beggars we encounter by chance on the streets to socializing our suffering to the person who has oppressed us for years, making our oppressor aware of the suffering he caused. Each encounter is an opportunity to love. If we make it a habit to give to those who ask, we are acting out of charity. We should not worry that they are falsely claiming their need. Those who defraud the generous will be dealt with harshly, if not in this life then the next. Those who innocently give to individuals who are taking advantage of their generosity will still be counted among the charitable and will build up heavenly currency. If we consistently act in charity, more will be infused in us. If we fail to act in charity, we will lose the ability to do so.

There will be times when we are asked to provide the words or resources that will change a person's life. In most of these situations we will be unconscious collaborators with God, having been put in the position that our natural reactions will provide just what the person needs at that particular time (CCC 307). But there are times we will be able to see the person's needs. If we have the opportunity to practice charity on their behalf, we should be grateful for the chance to participate in carrying out God's plan and to build up Heaven's currency. We should actively seek out these opportunities. If we let them go by, we not only have lost a chance to collaborate with God, but we have committed a sin of omission, because we are all called to love and alleviate suffering whenever we can. Loneliness is an exceptionally harsh way to suffer, so we should be particularly aware of the lonely, because we can all offer companionship.

This is doubly the case with relatives, whom we have a greater affinity to love. If we are estranged from any of them, it is incumbent on us to reach out and resolve the issues that are causing the problem. It is a shame when this occurs, and it is best to resolve the problem before it causes estrangement. Those who are close to you should love you the most, and you should love them out of charity. This can often mean sacrifice on the part of the one reaching out, but it is worth it to be charitable in all things, building up treasure in Heaven while at the same time improving your earthly relations.

If we look over the various types of loving relationships, we can see some common themes. In all our examples, God initiates love by putting us in the position to love. This is true regarding our love of self, our daily engagements with our spouses throughout our lives, and our relationships with family and friends. It is also true that in each of these cases we have the free will to love or not to love. Loving in all cases means putting others' needs before our own and having the desire to share in the life of the beloved.

Love is not static. The more we exercise our love through self-giving, the stronger the bonds that we create. Love also matures over time as we come to know our beloved better and as our knowledge of God and His goodness becomes more ingrained in our souls. However, if we fail to love when the opportunities arise, love can be lost. Finally, all these cases are predicated on loving the other because he or she is a child of God, regardless of whether it is the spouse God hand-picked for us to care for, a child entrusted to our care to raise, or a neighbor who is suffering and needs our aid.

When we love more consistently, we begin to feel joy as God gives us more infusions, motivating us to love more people and to love those we already love more deeply. As mentioned in the first chapter, this is the third task of suffering, to give us the opportunity and motivation to unleash our love of neighbor.

Through this process, we become more and more willing to sacrifice to make others' lives better and become more resistant to sin because we do not want to disappoint the God who is giving us consistent infusions of love. This is the fourth task of suffering, and it leads to redemption. This is where we spend the currency of the realm, by loving others to the point of self-sacrifice, which is to share in Christ's suffering for the good of souls.

Love is not a commodity to be counted; it is a capability that is measured in intensity. Having a lot of power, fame, or fortune does not increase the intensity of your love. Using your earthly resources to help others is charity. And divine charity requires more. To make it love, we must help others solely because doing so is right in the eyes of God. Jesus told us that if we give alms in order to be seen by others, we will get no spiritual benefit, because we have already received the reward we sought. He told us how to convert money into love — we must donate anonymously, and our Father, who sees in secret, will repay us (Matt. 6:1–4).

Jesus also taught that the real benefit from these transactions will go to those who give of themselves. Observing the people donating to the temple treasury, He called His disciples' attention to a poor widow's gift of two small coins. He explained that she was sacrificing what she had to live on and would suffer for the benefit of others, which is redemptive. He pointed out that she had given much more than the wealthy, who donated large sums out of their surpluses but didn't give enough of their wealth to suffer from it (Luke 21:1–4). Her love had grown so intense that she was willing to suffer for the benefit of the temple and the priests. The love of the wealthy members of the congregation was not intense enough for them to be willing to suffer — hence it was not redemptive.

It is possible and prudent to convert all of our earthly assets (money, fame, power, and whatever else you have tried to accumulate) to charity by putting them to use in aiding the least of our brothers. In fact, Jesus said if we do not come to the aid of those we encounter suffering, we will be condemned (Matt. 25:31–46). Anything of earthly value can be traded for love, but for us to derive spiritual benefit, we have to give to the point that it's a real sacrifice.

Giving to leave a legacy, or for any reason other than to do God's will, does not earn spiritual merit. Jesus said this explicitly in the Sermon on the Mount as just discussed (Matt. 6:1–6), and Jesus showed us the intensity of love required for Heaven when He was on the Cross.

It is also not enough to just give money. Katharine Drexel found that out when she proposed a new missionary order to help educate Native Americans and African Americans in the United States.[97] She went to Pope Leo XIII with the intention of funding the order. The pope was inspired to explain to her that she had to give of herself, not just money, to fulfill her place in God's plan, which would make her happy in both this life and the next. He told her to join the new mission and run it, which was indeed her place in God's plan since she was subsequently canonized a saint.

In the end, to be happy, we must be comfortable giving fully of ourselves and doing what is best for God's plan. During our lives, we are exposed to both the good and the bad and given the option to love, which means to support God and all of His plans, or to hate, which is to exploit our neighbors, doing only what is best for us. If we follow in the path of Jesus, we will be intensifying our love of God and avoiding mortal sin, which separates us from Him. If we have intensified our love of God to the point that we would never consider acting counter to His plans because we love Him and want what He wants, then we will be ushered directly into His Kingdom. If we spend our lives instead in the pursuit of transitory wealth, power, fame, or glory and do not convert our earthly treasure into heavenly currency by using it to alleviate human suffering, we will find ourselves lacking when we are judged. We will also find ourselves outside of the Kingdom we did not value highly enough during our lives, watching others on earth use all that we accumulated — some in a

---

[97] "St. Katherine Drexel," Catholic Online, https://www.catholic.org/saints/saint.php?saint_id=193.

wasteful way but others doing what we failed to do: converting the earthly wealth into Heaven's currency.

The good news is that we can change paths at any point before we die. We can convert our earthly wealth into heavenly currency by giving it to the needy. At the same time, we can ask forgiveness for our sins while taking our place in the Church, God's manifestation of His Kingdom on earth, thus building up the intensity of our love for God.

Charity, true theological love, is infused within us and is not something we can earn on our own. It is pure grace, a gift we can either accept or reject. The love of God relies on faith and hope for its existence. We cannot love a God we do not believe exists or we do not believe can save us. St. Thomas Aquinas asserts that "to love is indeed an act of the will tending to the good, but it adds a certain union with the beloved."[98] In the thought of St. Thomas, to love God is to recognize His goodness and to want to be part of it. That is all God is asking from us to avoid the fires of Hell. But to enter into the presence of God, the bar is higher. We need to be able to practice redemptive love, suffering for the benefit of others.

Building up the currency of love to pass this hurdle involves getting to know God. This can be done incrementally, with love growing as we build up prudence through suffering and align ourselves with God. Occasionally, when a person fails to heed their suffering, God uses a conversion event, with suffering so catastrophic that there is no question that only He can provide the remedy. If you recognize that you need God for your survival and He is sustaining you, you have recognized the good and should want to be part of that.

The way most people intensify their love sufficiently to avoid mortal sin and condemnation at the particular judgment is through the incremental trials that they get from the first task of suffering. Whenever they practice a vice, it will cause the sinner or the victim

---

[98]   *ST* II-II, q. 27, art. 2, resp. to obj. 2.

to suffer. When we start recognizing the choices that are free of suffering, we become prudent — we come to understand what God wants for us is happiness and we love Him for it.

We need, then, to have a love for God that is strong enough to help us avoid Hell but that also provides a base for the more substantial intensity of love required to enter Heaven. The more intense your love of God is when you enter Purgatory, the less time it should take for you to reach the required holiness needed for entry into Heaven (CCC 1030).

The Church summarizes the effects of charity in this way:

> The practice of all the virtues is animated and inspired by charity, which "binds everything together in perfect harmony"; it is the *form of the virtues*; it articulates and orders them among themselves; it is the source and the goal of their Christian practice. Charity upholds and purifies our human ability to love, and raises it to the supernatural perfection of divine love. (CCC 1827)

The fact that all love is from a common source with common attributes is perhaps explained best in conjunction with the Church as the Bride of Christ while also being the Body of Christ. If we act as the Bride of Christ, we are faithful and want the best for Jesus and all of God's children. We also desire to be united with God. Acting as the Body of Christ, we carry out His mission on earth, doing His will. This represents the merger of *eros* and *agape* love, which, in fact, become one and the same, as being faithful and wanting the best for God are synonymous with doing His will, which is also best for us.

The search for love is universal. People who are in love want it to last. People who have lost love seek to regain it, and if anyone on earth has not experienced love directly, they have certainly been exposed to it and want it for themselves. What many, if not most, fail to recognize and fully process is John's comment that "God is love"

(1 John 4:8), which makes it logically evident that searching for love is indeed searching for God.

Our journey through the meaning and power of love has shown us that all love originates with God through the infusion of charity. The individual with love "in his heart" is free to share that love with anyone he chooses or to let it go unused. To the extent that he shares with others the love he has received, he is doing God's work and will feel joy and the "spark" that we all feel as our souls bond with the souls of our beloved.

When we share our love with others, we give a part of ourselves to them. This is true, no matter who we love and in what type of relationship. Love always requires some sacrifice in time and resources that we will spend on our beloved, whether we are talking about spouses, children, siblings, parents, or the person we "randomly" encounter who needs our help. To love is to act divinely, to share in the divine nature.

To fail to share our love is to separate ourselves from God and His plan for us. This is going against our own best interests and will cause us to suffer "heartbreak." This is often the most intense type of suffering because it involves the tangible loss of the greatest good, Heaven's currency, which is the ability to love. Once we choose not to love, we begin to lose the capability. It is a case of "use it or lose it" as we separate ourselves from God.

If we want to love again, we need to seek out God, the source of love, and we need to purge our souls of the self-centeredness that kept us from sharing the love we had been given. Fortunately for us, God is always reaching out to us with opportunities to love, even to people who deny His existence. When one of these people falls in love and the bond is so strong that the person feels compelled to share himself with the beloved, then he is cooperating with God's plan. Love is the light that pierces the darkness of sin and self-centeredness and sets us on the path to righteousness.

Not only that, but love elevates our existence and leads to spiritual growth and the joy that accompanies it. Once we begin to love, it grows within us. This is manifested best in the marital relationship, which is naturally fruitful, producing children who are bonded to us and bring out the best in most people. Even in platonic *philia* relationships, as we become open to sharing ourselves with others, we will make more friends and love will grow. This makes us happy and healthy and motivates us to continue on the path that ultimately leads us to God and Heaven.

Once we begin to truly love our neighbors as ourselves, sharing the love that was shared with us, we become more open to loving God directly. Note that it is easier for most of us to love the individuals that God places before us because we can see their needs and those of our beloved and take tangible actions to meet them. God, on the other hand, is a spiritual being and has no needs to fulfill that He cannot fulfill Himself. Therefore, we love God by loving our neighbor and ourselves. This includes showing reverence to God and keeping the Sabbath holy, which are really for our benefit, not His.

It is true that people still have the opportunity to turn away from love, and some are hardened against it to a surprising degree, but love, like God, is all around us and is naturally appealing. St. Thomas says that all people are drawn to be their best selves because they want to be like God and with God.[99] We see this when people want to love, which is sharing in the divine nature.

What cannot be lost or understated is the capability of charity to produce joy. New love can be overwhelming. Those who are married no doubt remember the urgency they felt to be with their future spouse, and how, once meeting him or her, nothing felt right when they were not together. Any threat to that relationship was addressed

[99] *ST* I-II, q.2, Art. 8

with the utmost urgency, and the engagement and marriage were both joyous occasions as they made the spousal commitment clear.

In a similar way, those who have become parents and even grandparents will recall the joy at first meeting a newborn. The urge to hold and comfort him or her is exceptionally strong. Particularly telling is the ecstasy a new mother feels when she first holds the newborn after a hard and painful labor. In that moment, the joy of meeting the new love in her life washes away the pain and discomfort of the previous nine months. Fathers, although they may not feel the sense of relief that the labor is over to the same degree as their wives, will nonetheless feel joy at welcoming the new addition to the family, as will the older siblings, extended family members, and close friends.

All this can be lost, if we choose not to love, because it is, after all, an act of the will. However, God in His mercy, allows us to regain the ability to love. God is merciful in that He forgives prior error to those who repent. We see this in the sacrament of Reconciliation, in which the penitent confesses his sins to a priest, offers an act of contrition, and is absolved by the priest, who is acting in the person of Christ (CCC 1448). He does not offer salvation to the unrepentant sinner. In fact, God's use of punishment is to build up goodness, not to tear down a person. This is not possible if He affirms bad behavior (cooperating with evil), only if He uses His mercy to allow people to change. This is ultimately another way that God loves us. His correction through the confessional, which should also provide guidance on how to correct our behavior toward those we have failed to love, rebuilds our goodness and our ability to love both God and neighbor. It all begins with God, but man has agency, choosing to build love, Heaven's currency, by his actions and by reconciling with God when he fails to love.

CHAPTER 12

FINAL THOUGHTS

THIS CONCLUDES MY STUDY of the three mysteries that dominate human existence: suffering, death, and love. The three are fundamentally linked and could not exist in the same way without each other. Indeed, suffering and death are acts of God's love and, at the same time, are also instrumental in defining that love. The study of suffering, *Why All People Suffer*, came first because it showed how God loves us and dispelled the notion that suffering and God could not both exist.

Suffering is mysterious because it cannot be understood without charity, Heaven's currency, being its goal. Too often people see suffering only through the lens of human discomfort and miss the spiritual growth that it engenders. This is perhaps not that surprising, since physical ailments are accessible to the senses while we discern spiritual growth primarily through prayer, intellect, and faith.

Those who apply reason and faith to the question of why people suffer understand that suffering is a call to conversion. Suffering is a message from a loving God to avoid the evil that makes us uncomfortable and to embrace the charity that He offers. Indeed, true love entails self-giving that we demonstrate in the form of redemptive love. Jesus revealed the greatest love on the Cross, beckoning us to carry our own crosses with love and joy. Without self-giving, love is indistinguishable from attraction or friendship, because it is your willingness to suffer and give of yourself that ratifies the emotional bonds that make love real. God initiates love, but it is ultimately an act of human will that must maintain it. Love is a choice!

Dying without Fear, the second installment in this series, was a natural extension of *Why All People Suffer,* both in content and in my life journey. This second book allowed me to elaborate on dying and death far beyond what I did in the first book. The book was written while my mother, who was under my care, died and at a time when I was degrading physically from Parkinson's disease. This gave me both the impetus and practical experience that I lacked when I wrote *Why All People Suffer.* My contemplation led to research and new insights that I thought might benefit others. I focused more on God's plan for mankind and how dying and death played such an integral part in His plan. When I saw how God uses dying and death to draw us toward Himself, I became less terrified of them, and by understanding His love for us, I was no longer afraid of dying and death. These are important personal revelations for someone in my situation.

Also, for years I had been studying my family tree and had wanted to write a family history. I found a way to combine this with *Dying without Fear,* using examples from my family's death experiences to show how even very harsh lives and deaths could be seen in a positive light over time. I hope this use of family history will allow people to see God's love in their own cases, plus appeal to a larger audience.

Heaven's Currency is the culmination of the trilogy and is more expansive than my original idea. It began as a study of love, building on the theological concepts introduced in the first two books. The research and contemplation on this topic led me to understand that a search for love was a search for God. Writing *Heaven's Currency* helped me to better understand the role of God and the Church in our lives, which is to drive us to share in the divine nature and ultimately eternal life.

Love defines the goal of human life. Love is Heaven's currency. It is the only thing that transcends human death. Love is a capability that grows stronger with use, not a commodity that can be depleted. It gives death meaning because death marks the end of when you can build up the charity, divine love, that is needed to live eternally in God's Kingdom. Those who love with sufficient charity, accepting suffering for the good of another, will be admitted. In a very real way, you are building up godliness because God is love. If your love for others is not intense, you will be left outside the Kingdom, separated eternally from God, happiness, and joy.

Evil is the absence of God and love, and suffering is our God-given means of detecting it. Suffering motivates us to avoid evil and to seek out what we are missing, which ultimately is a manifestation of God. God is the source and summit of all that is good and all we desire, especially in the Holy Eucharist. When we experience evil and suffering, this is a gift of God, a sign of His love that shows He is drawing us to Himself. When we experience love, we are experiencing Him directly. Choosing to live eternally in God's love should not be a hard choice.

Just as Jesus described in the parable of the Prodigal Son, God wants us to dwell with Him forever in His heavenly home, although He forces no one to accept the invitation. It is our duty to store up treasures in Heaven while we live. These treasures are not stored in a material wealth "bank," but in charity. And God has instituted the sacraments to aid us throughout our lives so that we can love divinely.

When we reach this point, we conquer death because it no longer can cause fear in us. Just as we no longer desire our own will over the common good, we are no longer fearful of death, trusting in God's merciful promises of eternal life for those that follow Jesus, who has shown us the way back home to the Father.

This promise of eternal life is far more joyous than this valley of tears where evil and suffering provide a glimpse of what life will be outside the Kingdom. In the heavenly Kingdom, we will see God face-to-face, and all that is good and true directly from the infinite imagination of God. We will share the Beatific Vision with the most loving people who ever lived in their *perfected* state. We will never be bored or lonely again, and God will provide for all our needs, eliminating suffering.

The joy that is to be found in the heavenly Kingdom begins on earth as we conform ourselves more and more closely to God through prayer. This requires grace, and the result is the infusion of charity. As we love more, sharing in the divine nature, we grow spiritually, which we feel as joy. This is a touch of the divine to encourage us on the journey to righteousness and the Beatific Vision.

Whenever we are in the presence of Jesus, we experience the Kingdom of God. This occurs most readily in the Catholic Mass, where Jesus is present in the consecrated Eucharist, in the Word of God, in the person of the priest, and in the congregation, who collectively represent the Body of Christ. If we recognize all this, it will bring joy.

Those who approach the Church humbly, reflecting on her role as the Body of Christ and perhaps more as the Bride of Christ, whom He loves and protects with great tenderness and care, will understand that charity is the soul of the Church. Charity compels us to serve each other as we would serve Jesus Himself, for as He said, "Whatever you did for one of these least brothers of mine, you did for me" (Matt. 25:40). Acting in charity toward others increases our ability to do more, storing up treasure in Heaven where it can be used for entry into the Kingdom.

Our attitude toward the Church makes all the difference — that is, whether we "want to" versus "have to." When we seek to love and understand our brothers and sisters in Christ, they will become a blessing in our lives. This will be truer of the people we can help than the people who help us, although both will exist. Such is the way of charity and mutual self-giving. Some individuals wonder why certain people go to Mass every day without fail. It is because of the opportunity to get closer to Jesus and to His most devoted followers. Charity flows freely in such an environment, which I noticed after attending my first weekday Mass. Daily Mass was so compelling that I never wanted to stop attending, and that feeling has been with me for over twenty years.

To those desiring to advance in charity, get involved with your local parish in whatever capacity feels right and attend Mass as often as you can. Pray diligently and often. Do it out of love for God and a desire to do what is right and good. Remember, love that is self-giving is required for true divine charity, so do not hold back. Give everything you have, and it will be returned to you in abundance, not necessarily in this life but certainly in the next.

The other option involves doing the bare minimum for God. The Church lists five precepts, which represent the absolute minimum requirements for a Catholic to achieve growth in charity (CCC 2041–2043). They are the following:

1. Attend Mass on Sundays and Holy Days of Obligation and rest from servile labor.

2. Confess sins once per year.

3. Receive the Eucharist at least during the Easter season.

4. Observe the days of fast and abstinence established by the Church.

5. Help provide for the needs of the Church.

Perhaps many Catholics will be shocked to find that they are not doing even the minimum. This is far better than being shocked on Judgment Day. Still, God's mercy provides countless opportunities for conversion as long as we are alive.

If you are suffering in life, take heart because the Blessed Virgin Mary told St. Bernadette Soubirous, the visionary of Lourdes, on

February 18, 1858, "I don't promise to make you happy in this world but in the next."[100] God trains us through earthly suffering to share in the divine nature and a life of eternal joy. In His great mercy, God uses punishment to raise us up and never to destroy us.[101] He always has our best interest at heart. If we are open to following Him, we will experience His love, the currency of Heaven.

When we build up the Church, participating in her ministries and liturgies, and communicate with God through prayer, we bring the Kingdom of God ever closer. This is because we are actively answering His call for us to return to Him. We are building up our capability to act in charity, the currency of Heaven. We are purchasing the pearl of great price that Jesus talked about (Matt. 13:45–46). Once we understand its value, we will sell all we have to possess it. Willing to sacrifice our comfort for the good of another, we will take the proceeds and invest it to help the least of our brothers. We will not be afraid to do so, knowing that God cares for those who love Him (CCC 313). Having come to know God (faith), we will trust Him implicitly (hope) and love Him fully (charity). Having experienced redemptive love and built up the ability to practice charity, Heaven's currency, we will be ready to enter God's Kingdom and enjoy His company forever.

If the messages of *Heaven's Currency* seem daunting and you find yourself far from loving according to the divine nature, you are not alone. The saints probably felt the same way too. Loving divinely is to be like God, and that is beyond any human's innate ability. God knows this and will help us if we ask; however, He will not force us to practice charity. We must always remember that God loves us and does everything with our salvation in mind, including allowing suffering in our lives. We can learn from suffering by finding the good we lack, while at the same time

---

[100] "Apparitions," Lourdes Sanctuaire, http://www.lourdes-france.org/en/apparitions/.

[101] John Paul II, *Salvifici Doloris*, no. 7.

helping others. Suffering for others is redemptive, and it strengthens and expands our capability to love. Embracing our crosses and helping others carry theirs becomes easier and easier to do the more we practice it, because God's grace is never lacking. He desires to infuse His love into our hearts if we are willing to live according to His will.

I will leave you with this paradox: Following God's direction leads to happiness, while doing things our own way leads to sorrow. This is because God loves us, wants the best for us, and has a plan to achieve this. Since He is all-powerful and has perfect foresight, He designed the universe so that self-giving love is the answer to all of our problems and the cause of our happiness.

Those who do not know or trust God may resent their suffering, never recognizing that it is God directing them away from self-centeredness and the evil it engenders. If they "double down" and try to get what they want by exploiting others or try to mask the pain with the pleasures of this life, their suffering will only increase. This is God reaching out and motivating them to return to His Kingdom. Even if you find yourself in this type of death spiral, you can do as Garrett Johnson did and ask God for help.

As we see in the parable of the Prodigal Son, God eagerly waits for us in this life and in the next. We have only to return His love by choosing to love each other. If we love only ourselves, we will find ourselves alone in this life and isolated forever. If we are willing to sacrifice for each other's benefit, then we will all benefit. As St. John of the Cross once beautifully declared, "At the evening of life, you will be examined in love. Learn to love as God desires to be loved and abandon your own ways of acting. Love is the currency that pays the price of admission to enter Heaven, a currency backed by the blood of the Lamb."[102]

---

[102] John of the Cross, *The Collected Works of St. John of the Cross*, trans. Kieran Kavanaugh, O.C.D., and Otilio Rodriguez, O.C.D. (Washington, DC: ICS Publications, 1973), 672.

About the Author

Dr. Paul Chaloux was born in Maine in 1960, the eldest of six children. Educated in public schools, he earned a B.S. in chemical engineering from the University of Virginia and worked for IBM in Hopewell Junction, New York, as an engineer, manager, and strategist for more than thirty-three years. In 2014, Dr. Chaloux earned an M.A. in religious education from Fordham University, and in 2020, he earned a Ph.D. in moral theology from the Catholic University of America. Dr. Chaloux married his wife, Sue, more than thirty-five years ago, and they have four grown children and three granddaughters. He teaches theology at Catholic University, teaches online courses in suffering for the Avila Institute for Spiritual Direction, and serves as a catechist at St. Agnes Parish in Arlington, Virginia.

Sophia Institute

Sophia Institute is a nonprofit institution that seeks to nurture the spiritual, moral, and cultural life of souls and to spread the gospel of Christ in conformity with the authentic teachings of the Roman Catholic Church.

Sophia Institute Press fulfills this mission by offering translations, reprints, and new publications that afford readers a rich source of the enduring wisdom of mankind.

Sophia Institute also operates the popular online resource CatholicExchange.com. *Catholic Exchange* provides world news from a Catholic perspective as well as daily devotionals and articles that will help readers to grow in holiness and live a life consistent with the teachings of the Church.

In 2013, Sophia Institute launched Sophia Institute for Teachers to renew and rebuild Catholic culture through service to Catholic education. With the goal of nurturing the spiritual, moral, and cultural life of souls, and an abiding respect for the role and work of teachers, we strive to provide materials and programs that are at once enlightening to the mind and ennobling to the heart; faithful and complete, as well as useful and practical.

Sophia Institute gratefully recognizes the Solidarity Association for preserving and encouraging the growth of our apostolate over the course of many years. Without their generous and timely support, this book would not be in your hands.

www.SophiaInstitute.com
www.CatholicExchange.com
www.SophiaInstituteforTeachers.org

Sophia Institute Press® is a registered trademark of Sophia Institute.
Sophia Institute is a tax-exempt institution as defined by the
Internal Revenue Code, Section 501(c)(3). Tax ID 22-2548708.